One of my mother's most horrendous experiences was watching me swishing into one of her dinner parties at half-past ten at night aged about four, wearing my mother's long red wig, and her diaphragm perched jauntily on top of my head, saying to the bewildered guests, 'Hello, my name's Caraba of the East, how d'you like my hat?' Oddly enough, I found the wig last summer when I was pregnant and cleaning out drawers like a woman possessed, semi-naked because of the excessive heat, and about ninety stone overweight. Thrilled with my find, wearing the wig slapped on squiffily and covering one eye, I ran outside to find my husband. Unfortunately, I ran straight into our verger (we live next door to the church) who calmly engaged me in ordinary conversation as though I was normally dressed.

Our neighbours erected a large bird table outside their dining-room so that their baby son could watch the parade of birds feeding there each morning, while his mother told him all their names and chatted to him about each bird. He finally uttered his first word on a day when my friend's mother-in-law had popped round for tea. Gazing intently at her, he pointed and shouted, 'TIT'.

Paula Yates has published several books, and written for *Elle, Cosmopolitan*, the *Observer* and the *Sunday Times*. She has also appeared on more than thirty magazine covers. Her television career includes *The Tube*, and the series *Baby Baby*. In 1985 and 1986 she won the Gold Award from the New York Film and Television Festival for the best documentary interview. She lives in Kent and London where she does all her work during naptimes – the children's, not hers. Her favourite occupation is lying in the long grass with the children, eating fig rolls.

The Fun Don't Stop

Loads of rip-roaring activities for you and your toddler

PAULA YATES

PAN BOOKS

LONDON, SYDNEY AND AUCKLAND

First published 1991 by Bloomsbury Publishing Limited

This edition published 1993 by Pan Books Limited
a division of Pan Macmillan Publishers Limited
Cavaye Place London SW10 9PG
and Basingstoke

Associated companies throughout the world

ISBN 0 330 31780 6

Illustrations by Natacha Ledwidge

1 3 5 7 9 8 6 4 2

A CIP catalogue record for this book, is available from
the British Library

Printed and bound in Great Britain by
Cox & Wyman Ltd, Reading

This book is dedicated to Little Pixie, who is my inspiration and without whom this book would have been finished in half the time; also with all my love to Anita for all of her support and help.

Contents

To be Queen Elizabeth within a definite area, deciding sales, banquets, labours and holidays; to be Whiteley within a certain area, providing toys, boots, sheets, cakes and books; to be Aristotle within a certain area, teaching morals, theology and hygiene; I can understand how this might exhaust the mind, but I cannot imagine how it would narrow it. How can it be a large career to tell other people's children about the Rule of Three and a small career to tell one's own children about the universe? How can it be broad to be the same thing to everyone and narrow to be everything to someone? No; a woman's function is laborious because it is gigantic, not because it is minute.

– G. K. CHESTERTON, 'On Being a Mother at Home . . .'

INTRODUCTION

I always wanted to be one of those mothers like Aunt Fanny in the *Famous Five* books. In my dreams I was Aunt Fanny with my hair in a sausage around my head, a flowered dress that drooped at the hem, and five shining children, living in a gloriously English forties house with french windows and rolling lawns, and one of those maids called a tweeny. I would be in the garden with a basket, clipping roses, occasionally drifting indoors to prepare vast picnics of cakes and ginger beer ... sometimes I saw myself, still with the five shining children in tow, on the brow of a hill, an iridescent blue sky filled with blustery white clouds above us – a veritable Laura Knight painting. In my secret dream of motherhood at no point do the children utter the dreaded phrase 'I'm bored', and one of them is *not* applying bubble gum to her sister's fringe with a pair of pliers...

Someone told me recently that they could always identify the mothers of older children because those mothers were the ones who managed to wear lipstick. I think this is pertinent to the gap between my vision of myself as a latter-day Aunt Fanny and the reality. The sausage isn't just wrapped round my head – all of me resembles a *bratwurst*; I droop more than the hem of the flowery dress; and I seem to have acquired a distressing likeness to Lettuce Leaf, the ugliest girl in the school, who wore her lank hair in a centre parting with two hair-grips forcing it into submission.

In my fantasies I never saw myself falling asleep on the floor before the opening titles of *LA Law* floated on to the screen. I didn't see months passing before I could speak to my closest girlfriends, all adult conversation being continually interrupted by my two year old doing things like practising an arcane form of medical research on her little sister in a secluded corner around the back of the Puff-O-Matic washing machine.

Despite the relentless demands of babies and toddlers, I do still retain a wistful belief that it is possible to leave one's children with blissful memories of childhood. And because all that we remember are fragments, moments, seconds, they should be idyllic, happy ones. Discovering the world around her at her mother's side – experiencing something as simple as the first touch of a rabbit's fur, the first long hot day of summer spent eating strawberries on a farm – can leave a lasting impression on a child, and help her to form a sense of the world as a secure, loving, if mysterious place.

Of course in order to be really like Aunt Fanny you have to turn yourself into a rather heady cross between Joyce Grenfell and a Butlin's redcoat, baking, trilling songs from all the old hit musicals, keeping the house from looking exactly like the Titanic mid-plummet, not rashly breaking off contact with all your single friends simply because they wear clean clothes and don't have a tummy that looks like Skegness sands at low tide.

When I wrote my last book, *The Fun Starts Here*, I was heavily pregnant with my third daughter Pixie. I had two other delicious daughters and didn't realise how easy it was with only a couple of children. In fact I'd had an easy time of almost everything. Perfect births where party poppers sailed into the air with every push. The baby finally shooting across the room at high velocity, while all the rest of the family milled around the bed looking supportive at the same time as never averting their gaze from the bedside lamp. By the time the tea had arrived, I was back to my old weight and wearing a sequined sheath and writing three novels. Now things have changed – I'm still wearing my stomach as a sarong and pretending I got it from Donna Karan in the January sales. I've experienced terminal writer's block, a difficult birth and the battle to maintain my sexuality while in possession of an off-white, triple-D cup Mothercare maternity bra, a garment which arrives guaranteed to give you all the allure of a maggot . . .

Once you have more than two children you suddenly need the tactics of Rommel to actually get out of the house, let alone reaching the park and being wildly enthusiastic and nurturing in the open air. During the snowy weather everyone in our family had to wear 300 layers topped off by a quilted snowsuit secured with a combination lock that would have baffled Butch Cassidy. Invariably, I would get them all herded to the top of the street, singing songs from Brownie camp in a crazed fashion, only to discover that one member of the merry band had filled their nappy to capacity, while another one had toppled headlong into the only puddle within a ten-mile radius.

This kind of mundane, everyday harassment can either turn you into a serial killer or teach you some compassion ... The time spent trudging back home through the frozen wastes to change the nappy again also gives one the chance to fine-hone the many clichés it's tempting to trot out to your husband when he gets home: *You'd all miss me if I was dead, You don't know what it's like when you're not here*, or the pathetic, *Your children have ruined me*, which is best uttered while sitting forlornly on the end of the bed looking down at your stomach as it cascades over your M&S drawers fetchingly topped off with the Mothercare maternity bra ... Put it this way – carry on wearing them and you may not have to worry about giving any more children idyllic childhood memories of groping rabbit droppings ...

Being an at-home, hands-on mother of the old-fashioned sort also makes you realise that one old saying is absolutely true – the devil does make work for idle small hands. Yesterday I was on the phone for marginally longer than my normal three and a half seconds when I became aware of an eerie silence all over the house. As there is never any silence in our house, most of my life had passed in front of my eyes by the time I made it to the sitting-room, where my daughter Peaches was standing naked (except for her red gumboots) surveying her handiwork. She'd spread the entire carpet with water-resistant bum cream, which made it feel as though I was walking across freshly plucked liver.

Babies and toddlers are incredibly hard work, and not for the reasons that are often given when people are pitying stay-at-home mothers for the stultifying, mind-numbing existence they must be enduring. Children learn more in the first five years of their lives than in the whole of the following fifty. In order to manage this feat they are voracious for information, crazed with longing to investigate their environment (which is a polite way of saying they do things like flinging your perfume down the loo), and they don't want to watch TV and vegetate in isolation. They want to be with *you*, indoors and outdoors; they want to play, sing, dance, make things and talk all the time. None of this leaves any mother with much time for things that previously she would have regarded as basics of life like baths alone occasionally. Small children need constant surveillance, entertainment, stimulation, and soothing from their mothers; this, combined with maintaining a sense of self, a home, perhaps a part-time career, and a relationship, is bewilderingly tiring for most.

Tiring but not stultifying . . .

The media has a tendency to perpetuate two great myths: the first is that mothers today who have made the decision to stay at home and make sacrifices are trapped in a repetitious, isolated existence with NO FUN EVER, and the second is that only working mothers have to juggle their lives while tripping precariously along the career/ home highwire. The working mother is portrayed as wearing shell-pink sateen camiknickers under a business suit while she's on the portable phone to President Bush who's just rung her to ask what to do next about the Gulf, and when she *is* at home she spends her time rucking with the nanny about whether nanny can have a weekend off.

But in many ways it is women at home who have a far harder juggle to manage – their lives are not so clearly delineated as those who leave each morning for a job; they must try to accommodate the needs of both children and husband while at the same time trying to make space to indulge their own whims, like wanting to lie on the sofa drinking pints of Guinness and watching Australian soap operas about rampant bush rangers.

If you are attempting to work at home too that can increase the stress, as it is a difficult feat to pull off when your children are very small – unless you happen to enjoy staying up until two in the morning all the time. I'm writing this book in the early hours of the mornings and frequently find myself typing fluent jabberwocky.

And being at home isn't very glamorous. It's all very well to sneer at those who hanker for glamour, but I think that everyone does sometimes, and it's hard to feel a Jezebel when you are semi-conscious on the sofa at seven-fifteen every evening.

*

Talk to almost any mother who is spending all her time at home with her toddler and you're likely to discover that sometimes both of them feel bored – with their familiar surroundings, with each other and their daily routine, with the same toys and books. What I aim to do here is suggest many different activities from which to choose for those times when the day seems to be stretching ahead and you've run out of inspiration. I've tried all of them on my kids: when we've felt isolated and getting out and about has seemed a daunting prospect; on days when I've had a friend coming over and I've wanted some time to talk uninterrupted; on days when I've felt too tired and grumpy to be hilarious and vibrant for everyone; on rainy days and on days when other children were popping over (and in order to prevent the entire home from being demolished). They're ideas for things to do to keep everyone happy, quietly or not so quietly.

Children learn so much through their play and we can derive so much pleasure from watching them and playing with them. There is the added bonus that children with a lot to do are much easier to live with than the ones who are loitering about looking shifty. Activities may sound like something girls in orange dungarees do on children's TV, but really they are an excellent way of breaking up the day and giving children something to discuss and look forward to.

My own parents were not keen on activities at all, a reaction to their own parents pushing them. In my father's case he was tied to a piano from the age of six, and spent most of his teenage years rising out of pits in cinemas in various parts of the country, furiously playing his organ, and grinning wildly. My mother was sent to dancing classes almost as soon as she could stand up, and then spent her teenage years slapping her thigh playing principal boys in the Blackpool pantos, until finally she could slap no more and ran away to Paris with nothing but a five-pound note and a lilac feather boa. Consequently, my mother's idea of an activity when I was a child was to lay out a plate of cold meats and let me arrange them for teatime.

So when I was little I devoured Enid Blyton books and was sickeningly jealous of all her child characters who had these wonderful, patient parents who never hit-flicked them around the head with a pair of wet tights, and who were always dead keen to go owl spotting. Fifty years after the books were first published my own daughter reads them and longs for the same treats, or at least the same level of input from me.

So here it is: the guide to being an Enid Blyton mythical mother!

Chapter One

All Aboard
for
Playtime

Along with kissing and eating, playing is the most important thing in your baby's life. It's impossible to emphasise enough the importance of talking and playing with your baby from the moment she is born – play is her way of defining the world around her and understanding what she sees, her way of discovering the potential of her five senses and, when you think that new babies don't yet know where you end and they begin, and jump if they spot their foot popping up into view, they have a lot of new things to take in.

Babies like really goofy things. People who aren't used to being around them feel thoroughly sheepish about it. Pixie adores what my husband rather unkindly refers to as my 'twat's voice', which I prefer to think of as a special loving tone interspersed with billing and cooing noises. One of the things that many new parents find a little disconcerting is suddenly being expected to be able to recite the whole of 'Mother Goose' to a musical accompaniment, standing on one's head, possibly juggling or blowing bubbles at the same time. Babies adore the theatrical, that's why you'll notice that when friends who already have children come to see you they immediately fall into their patter, leaving your normally quiet baby shrieking and chortling while you sit pea-green with envy near by vowing to copy it all once they've left.

Pixie likes playing Peepo! and Boo, and being thrown into the air – at five months old she can grasp well at objects held out for her. Her older sister, who is two, likes sophisticated games – make-believe, endless mummying games where she breast-feeds her doll for hours, nursery rhymes, songs, and story books. She also likes a nostalgic game of Peepo! or Boo with her baby sister.

A lot of books about play have a great deal about different toys in them, and all the problems for the modern mother that come with toys. Will my son furiously deface bus shelters if I let him have a gun for his birthday? for example. I have a friend who was determined not to allow her son to have a gun of any kind to play with and was then horrified to find that he was chasing around in the garden with his friends firing at them with a courgette. Children will make up games and create toys and improvise furiously if need be.

Sexism is another great worry, but one thing seems to be true: girls are sometimes willing to play with 'boyish' toys and with a group of small boys without being worried about appearing tomboyish, but most small boys (even very small boys) will go pale-grey at the idea of playing, say, Hairdressers, even if they are cast in the leading role of Pierre de Finchley. So you may find that you can get your daughter interested in a combine harvester, and your son will, in the privacy of his own home, probably don an apron (not floral) for some baking, but in general I've noticed that most children are ASTOUNDINGLY sexist without any conditioning or prompting whatever.

Yesterday I was in a taxi and the driver was bemoaning the fact that he had spent a great deal of money on a birthday present for his four year old, only to find him indulging in that predictable behaviour, sitting in the box all afternoon and then spending the evening untying the knot on the ribbon that had been around the wrapping paper.

Most parents realise that they buy their children too many toys, and, if your child is allowed to watch TV, she will be subjected to an endless stream of adverts for mini Ferraris and other useless things. Having said that, our house is littered with Barbie's lingerie, and huge piles of disgustingly scented My Little Ponies.

I once did a film for the BBC at the My Little Pony factory. I only agreed to do the film because I wanted Fifi to see how the horrible little beasts were made. We were told that the Ponies were the result of six years' market research into what little girls like most, namely horses, and brushing hair – hence Pony's glamorous appearance.

Someone I know once had to ring up Bonnie Langford and ask her if she had anything odd in her garden for a magazine feature.

'Oh yes,' she trilled happily, 'I've got a darling little Wendyhouse.'
My friend replied that that didn't seem a very odd thing to have in one's garden at all.

'It is if you're twenty-three,' came the terse reply . . .

The other day I was talking to someone about the things she liked playing with best when she was a child. She told me there were two; the first was an eight-foot-deep hole that her mother dug in their back garden, in which the whole family played all summer long; and the second was a huge cardboard box that her father's lawnmower came in. She played in the box in the kitchen until it finally disintegrated. Neither of these were really 'toys' but they were what had made the greatest impression.

As long as you always supervise your child, and lay down lots of foam for her to fall on to, almost anything can be the basis of an indoor adventure: a long tablecloth can transform a table into a den; a clothes-horse is another good base for den building. Some very old, large chests have enough room on top for a little hut to be constructed with a ladder leading up to it.

Most toddlers aren't heavy enough to damage your home! If you are good at DIY you might think about putting some heavy-duty hooks into the ceiling joists and beams so that you can have a rope ladder, or a small swing, inside your house. A wooden plank down the stairs, or off the side of the sofa, makes an adequate slide. The corners of your plank need to be rounded, and the whole thing should be sanded down and then varnished to avoid splintered bums. It can also be used as a see-saw, and for jumping off and on to, or over. If you have a garden, don't forget what my friend said about the joys of a big hole to play in, though!

Of course, you can't be devising exciting play-opportunities all the time! Everybody has bad days, and sometimes I think it's best not to try to be supermother, but to admit defeat when things aren't working out and you feel tired or fed up. You'll find that one of the horrible truths about being a mother is that everyone around you is a litmus paper for your moods. The worse snit you are in, the more fractious and difficult your children will be, so days like this can be a vicious circle and end with you feeling grumpy and guilty and the children miserable.

THE FUN DON'T STOP

If you're not in the mood for going out and being sociable, or even making it to the swings, just leave it for the day, stay in, get cosy and comfortable, and allow yourselves to while away your day in a different way. Watch TV, even if you don't normally allow it; rent a video and curl up on the sofa together; or get out all the toys and play with them. If it's a *really* rotten day, get into bed with a pile of your child's favourite books and enjoy them together with a potent joss stick burning, a fire in the grate, and a large scarf draped over the bedside lamp. The two of you will feel as though you are in the casbah, and forget that you started out tetchy!

CHOOSING THE RIGHT TOYS

Two to four months For a passive little baby the first realisation that she can actually make something happen must be a great leap – when she realises that by moving her body she can make her bouncy chair move. At about two months old she will begin to try to swipe at objects and kick up at them with her feet if she's lying down. Your house will suddenly be full of mobiles and objects on strings. And you can encourage your baby to get the idea by guiding her hands towards the objects to see that she can make them swing around by knocking them.

Buy a baby gym, which is a frame with dangly bits on it, or create your own, constantly changing one. Try tying a balloon on to it; balloons send my daughter Pixie into a frenzy, as she is firmly convinced that they are some sort of airborne bosom which she longs to cram into her face. Or try the foil dish that housed the last Mr Kipling cake you surreptitiously ate; a crackly brown paper bag; a long sock filled with newspaper bells; in fact, anything that makes a noise when a successful flail is made.

Even if she's not attempting to swipe at them, a baby will enjoy looking at mobiles, and it's a good idea to hang them above the changing mat – babies get cheesed off with being endlessly changed and a mobile relieves the monotony. I made one for Fifi that was simply long strips of silver kitchen foil attached to the ceiling with drawingpins. I then ran a knife down the foil strips to make them into long curls that wiggled around.

A more ambitious mobile can be made by hanging a coat-hanger from the ceiling and hanging objects from that, for example, a load of foil bottle tops; Christmas tree decorations; coloured feathers; anything you think will be interesting to gaze at. In our kitchen we have a large moon and star made of cardboard and covered in thick silver glitter. The mobile is surrounded by strings of fairy lights in the shape of red-hot chilli peppers! This is startling and gripping stuff if you're three months old.

Four to six months By four months your baby will have started to reach out and grab at things, and will be learning to control her arm movements. Slowly but surely she will be achieving visual-motor co-ordination – which means that as she sees something her hand will reach towards it. After this stage, she will get hold of objects and put everything into her mouth to further investigate with her sensitive mouth.

If you have rattles to go across her bouncy chair it's a good idea to put them on, as this will encourage her to reach out to the rattle, and help her to understand that she is making the chair bounce too.

You may want to make rattles for her to play with. Fill any container with a child-proof lid with pebbles, rice, pasta shells, lentils, or seeds. The noise made by her rattle will help your baby connect it with what is in her hand.

There were two small things that my children found entertaining when they were still at the stage of lying on the floor pretending to be a fur rug. One was a pair of baby socks with bells sewn tightly into each toe and a face embroidered on the foot, so that when my daughters played with their feet there was something interesting there. (They didn't wear these socks all the time, I hasten to add!) The other was a sheet of brightly coloured wrapping paper, which all babies like to look at or tussle with to the death. (Older babies will attempt to eat the paper, giving you a heart-attack, and remember never to give a baby newsprint, because it's slightly toxic.)

You can buy baby activity mats with differently textured cloths sewn on to them, but why not provide your baby with a little basket filled with furry, cold, soft, and slippery fabrics for her to experiment with.

Six to eight months By this time your baby will have increased her manipulative skills so that she is able to pass a toy from one hand to the other. You can help her to develop these skills in various ways: by giving her larger or heavier toys than usual that require two hands to hold them; by giving her another toy to hold so that eventually she can hold two things without dropping them; by offering books or toys to her in a way that means that she has to think about which is the easiest way to grip them. Learning to hold two objects is very important – before, your baby would have just dropped the first one to clutch at the second, but once she is holding the two she'll soon start to realise that she can also use her two HANDS together for games. Now is the time to get out your old nursery rhyme book and swot up on all the ones like 'Pat a Cake' that involve clapping.

Eight to twelve months Lots of things will have changed by the first birthday. Instead of your baby just watching you playing, instead of her gazing in wonder at her siblings' toys and stuffing them into her mouth, she will begin to control her playing time, and to initiate the games she finds most fun.

By about ten months, babies are able to let go deliberately. Once your baby can do this, you can play simple 'giving' games with toys which she'll give back to you. You can also start to play simple games of ball. She will need to sit with her legs apart on the floor while you very gently roll the ball between her legs: she will then start to try to push the ball away for you to 'catch'.

Babies *love dropping things*! Now that your baby realises that she can let go of things, she'll be keen to develop this new skill herself and drop toys over the edge of her pushchair, high chair, bath, and cot – continuously, until you are on all-fours, purple in the face, and saying pathetically that this isn't fun any more. Maybe the first 300 times was fun, but not now. It is also a social game to your baby because she will enjoy the interaction with you – she throws and you pick up, even if you feel fed up after a while.

My elder daughters have both been champion sorters at this age. I think lots of babies do go through a phase where every bookshelf is an open invitation to a furious sorting session. When Fifi was at it, books used to actually fly over her shoulder as though she were a mad professor looking for theorems under the bed. If your child develops a passion for sorting, emptying, and filling up boxes, then provide her with one, as it can send anyone almost demented having their handbag, make-up bag, and drawers rifled through regularly.

In the kitchen we let Peaches have one cupboard at ground level filled with empty boxes and containers to sort through and rearrange, while I cooked. Another good idea is to provide plenty of containers that fit into one another and things to put into them like carrots, nappies, and playing cards (actually, cards are a bit of a pain if you find you're always the one picking them up again!). A large plastic teaset or cooking set is a good buy at this point.

One to two years Most toddlers (as your baby now is!) find it hard to walk at your pace. Once you have wheeled her to the park or carried her there in the sling, grab the chance to lie on the grass resting (all mothers should take any opportunity to lie prone, or in a heap) while your child waddles about investigating and enjoying new freedom.

You might want to get some bean bags from a toy shop. Lots of small toddlers still like throwing and fetching games. You could make your own bean bags from lurid remnants of fabric and some beans for weight. Also good for improving co-ordination and balance are pull-along toys – make sure they are wide enough, otherwise they tend to fall over and be deeply boring. I made one out of a shoebox: I attached a string to pull it along by, and stuck two ears on the front.

From one to eighteen months, a toddler will enjoy picture books filled with photographs of familiar objects and animals; all kinds of bath toys like ducks, boats and squirters; a toy telephone (the noisier the better); stacking, threading and nesting toys; wooden blocks; and toy houses with little people inside.

On the investment front, a small climbing frame with a slide is a lasting toy, so are little trucks a toddler can sit on and ride and store blocks in.

An eighteen-month-old child will have moved on to shape-sorting toys; and push-along toys – all kinds, from doll's prams to something more elaborate!

Two to three years A two year old will long for Play-Doh and a real bike, even if she can't actually pedal it yet; a Wendyhouse; a garage with cars and trucks or tractors or diggers; and sturdy wooden puzzles that have pieces with handles that can be lifted up to reveal another drawing underneath.

By two and a half your child will be playing quite complicated acting-out games like Shops, or Tea parties. She will be enjoying dressing-up games; wooden puzzles with large pieces; a simple train set; and construction toys like Duplo, the 'baby' Lego.

By three a child will enjoy playing with a wheelbarrow; riding a tricycle and a truck that she can pedal; toy tools; household equipment in miniature; and puppets, dolls, and teddies. Bubbles; balls; art equipment; and buckets and spades will also go down well.

Four to five This is the age when your child will be engrossed in learning many more skills, and becoming more competent physically. Small rackets and balls and anything that encourages sport will be popular. A big cardboard clock-face for learning to tell the time will be appreciated, as will toys for imaginary games like toy money and a toy shop; a dressing-up outfit like a nurse's uniform, cowboy or fairy costume. Your child's interest in books will be growing, and she'll enjoy simple board games like Ludo, Snakes and Ladders, and draughts. A skipping rope will be relished, and a swing is a good idea if you're feeling extravagant. Furiously encourage any interest in music with tapes and a junior tape machine, a kazoo or harmonica or other small musical instrument.

How to know if a toy is safe Every year children are injured, sometimes fatally, by rogue toys that do not fit the British standards for safety – but which may have seemed like bargains to the parents who bought them. Sometimes cheap imported toys from countries with no regulations get into Britain, and are sold by traders who only want to make money and don't care about quality.

A toy that does conform to the standards has a lion on it, confirming that it meets the British Standard 5665. But you still have to check it yourself, and even home-made toys can be hazardous. Make sure the toy is fire resistant; has no sharp wires in it and has embroidered features. If it does have attached eyes they should be secured with a safety-lock, and arms and legs should be stitched on firmly. Make sure the toy doesn't have long threads for hair, or tassels, or loose bits hanging off it.

There are certain guidelines that you should try to follow at home to make sure life with toys is safer for your children: test toys for sharp edges; test wheels to make sure they are on securely; make sure children don't go near batteries; and *never* let a child put a toy with a clockwork motor near her hair – the toy can get tangled up

in it and pull the hair out in a clump. Throw away all damaged toys
– sometimes they can be dangerous. If your child is given a toy gun,
make sure she understands that any toy gun must be fired *away*
from people. Toys should never be left on the stairs for little people
to trip over. Babies are in need of special toys – washable, and with
no small parts they could choke on.

Join a toy library If there's a toy you'd particularly like to try on your
child, but can't find it in the shops, or can't afford it, then you might
be able to get hold of it through your local toy library. Or set up
your own borrowing system by swapping some of your children's
toys with a friend's children's toys. That way, no one gets bored!

PLAYING WITH WORDS

The speed with which children learn to talk varies enormously – my daughter Fifi could speak a few words at thirteen months but her sister was able to converse fairly fluently at the same age, so it's worth bearing in mind that talking early has no relevance to what your child will be able to do later on. Having said that, living with a child who can understand and talk to you early does make a parent's life much easier, I've found – I've been able to ask Peaches what was wrong with her when she has felt ill, and to reason with her when she's been lying on the floor in Waitrose the same colour as a jar of pickled cabbage and kicking her legs up and down. It's obvious that increased communication between you is bound to make for an easier time.

Our neighbours erected a large bird table outside their dining-room so that their baby son could watch the parade of birds feeding there each morning, while his mother told him all their names and chatted to him about each bird. He finally uttered his first word on a day when my friend's mother-in-law had popped round for tea. Gazing intently at her, he pointed and shouted, 'TIT'.

Keep up the chat Your child will have started to pick up language and facial expressions a long time before she actually begins to talk – all the time you have spent looking at her and chatting to her will have seen to that. Even the silliest games are important: just sitting saying shaming things like 'Wooji-wooji-wooji' (approved in our household). You say it to your baby whilst smiling at her, she responds by smiling back at you, and the smile is so adorable she sees that you enjoyed it and responded to what she just did. This is a feeling of control for a small baby and a first step towards conversation and verbal communication.

When you are talking to your baby there are a few tricks you can use to help her: exaggerating your voice and facial expressions and using wild gestures, for example. Parents often sound rather like the British on holiday who converse on the assumption that anyone south of Clacton will understand English as long as it is spoken very loudly and an 'O' is added on to the end of pertinent words. It's a good idea to use your baby's name instead of 'you' or 'yours': 'Fifi's dolly', for example. Chat to your baby about the things she is interested in: the cat, the park, food, toys, bathtime, her siblings, the trees and flowers.

When you are telling her a bedtime story or just having a story on the sofa to relax together, encourage her to insert sound-effects at pertinent moments: miaows, shrieks, and farmyard noises are all good for encouraging your child to listen intently to the story and to vocalise. Try not to be tempted to correct wrong pronunciations, and obviously the harder you attempt to understand what your child is telling you, the more encouraged she will be to try again. All of my children have invented words – Peaches called aeroplanes 'daboodangs' and Fifi insisted on calling shoes 'noo-aaas'. We still occasionally lapse into nostalgic chat in our secret family language.

You can help your child to increase her vocabulary by pointing things out and naming them, and by introducing new sights and activities into your conversation. You might feel a bit like Peter O'Sullivan doing the racing commentary but it's all for a good cause! When you are chatting, don't feel that you have to over-simplify your normal speech patterns. Talking a bit more slowly might help, but a baby understands much more than she can say and anyway learns to speak by listening to proper speech. Initially of course she's not going to have perfect grammar, and a sentence may take some time to come out, but it's worth the wait.

Mirror talk Most babies are thrilled by looking at themselves in the mirror; they turn into miniature Gloria Swansons and can be encouraged to chat into the mirror. Sit with your baby in front of a mirror and play a simple game of pointing. Point to her nose and say, 'This is your nose,' then, 'This is Mummy's nose; this is your tummy; this is Mummy's fifteen rolls of tummy,' and so on...

Hear that rhythm Singing to your baby and repeating rhymes will help her to get an impression of the rhythm of language. The rhymes that have actions to go with them also help to give your baby clues as to what words mean so that she can start to associate words with actions. Small babies really do enjoy rhymes and songs of all kinds long before they know what you're actually on about. So, you might try 'See-saw, Margery Daw' or 'Round and Round the Garden', or gently singing 'Row, Row, Row Your Boat'.

Hide and seek A mobile baby can learn new words by playing fetching games – you ask her to fetch things from around the room. Eventually you could play a game of hunt the object, but you have to let the baby see where you are hiding it, and will probably always need to hide the treasure in the same place.

WATER PLAY

All babies can be water nymphs, and every child has it in her to be a perfect Esther Williams, although probably on her first trip to the local baths you may suspect you have more of an Esther Rantzen. Water inspires endless possibilities for play and discovery and mess!

You shouldn't leave a child playing with water unsupervised simply because a toddler can drown in the most minute amounts of water. You have to hover near by, and you have to put up with lots of water being sloshed around, but the entertainment value is enormous – and you can follow water play up with water-inspired reading and crafts.

In the bath It's wise to avoid ructions by emphasising that slapping large amounts of water down the walls is *verboten*, as is standing up in the bath, because a small person will topple over in the water and knock her head on the taps. Fifi of course did this – she looked like Joe Frazier's left buttock, which was unfortunate as she was about to be a bridesmaid.

The bath is an excellent place for water play, but don't restrict water play to bathtime – it is a marvellous way of relaxing young children at any time of the day – especially if you've just come in from a harrowing shopping expedition.

At the sink Let your toddler stand on a chair by the sink and play at washing up, pouring out, and splashing about. Remember, though, to put an old towel under the chair to stop it from slipping. Or you can put the washing-up bowl on to the floor, and again you'll need to put a lot of old towels or a rubber sheet down as there are bound to be considerable spills.

Inevitably, clothes will get wet; either put a large plastic play-apron on your child, one of the sort that has sleeves in it, or if it's a hot day, she could play without any clothes on.

In the garden In the summer, it's fun to play with water out in the garden, in which case you could use a hosepipe and sprinkler as well (unless like we do you live in Kent, where there's a permanent water shortage on a scale with the water shortage in the wilds of Arizona, and hosepipes are banned under threat of 300 years in prison).

Your child may be at the age to enjoy copying the things that you do in which case she'll like washing her trucks or her dolls' hair. Or she may just enjoy flinging the water around, watching it drip through a collander, squirting it out of an empty washing-up liquid bottle, pouring it out of a jug on to her toys, or simply pouring water from one container to another. To add further interest you might like to colour the play water with food dyes, or even add some bubble bath so that she gets clean while she plays!

Have fun in the garden with a sinking and floating game. You'll need a large container for the water, perhaps a baby bath or an old fish tank – and colour the water if you wish. Throw in lots of different objects, such as sponges, straws, tea strainers, sieves, ping-pong balls. The idea is to guess which objects will sink and which will float. Children also enjoy talking about what the different objects feel like, and will fiddle around for hours with them in the water. Get the children to close their eyes and guess what is underwater.

WATERY CREATIONS

Boats for the local pond A great boat that floats can be made from an empty milk carton, or even a large matchbox, with drinking straws and lolly sticks for masts. Or you could use an empty container from your last Chinese take-away – but it needs to be carefully wrapped in masking tape to ensure that it floats. Paint very brightly coloured sails, and attach a long string so that the boat can be pulled along.

Slimy stuff To make slime you need a cup of soap-flakes; 2 l. warm water; a couple of egg beaters, and, if you want to colour it, some food colouring too. Dissolve the soap-flakes in the water in your large washing-up bowl, and then leave the mixture to stand until it becomes thick and ready for the children to beat with the egg beaters after adding a little colouring. Provide a selection of kitchen utensils for pouring, scooping and measuring. Squeezing the mixture through a sponge is fun, too.

Even worse slimy stuff This really is an outdoor pursuit. Just mix two packets of cornflour to two large cups of water, and add a little colouring. Put a long strip of wallpaper lining-paper on the grass, and make swirling patterns on it with the paste. Best of all, your child will want to talk to you about how the slimy cold mixture feels! You could find yourselves having a sixties happening right in your own back yard!

Coloured icecubes This is another simple idea that is plenty of fun – just put a few drops of food dye into the water and then freeze it in several differently sized containers. When the cubes are ready put the smaller ones into glasses of lemonade, and the larger ones into a big bowl of water for your child to play with.

NEVER THROW AWAY A BOX ONCE YOU HAVE CHILDREN!

No matter whether it is a little box that came with the cereal selection or a massive huge box that contained a piece of cleaning equipment or was left by the removal men, all toddlers love a good box. A box can be all things to all toddlers. Small boxes are good for keeping treasures in, and then shaking to listen to the noises they make; small boxes are good for putting into big boxes like Russian dolls. If you've had the presence of mind to pack your few groceries into massive boxes (much to the astonishment of the assistants in Sainsbury's as they eye your three bananas and a turnip) the world is your oyster ...

Your box can be ... Painted like a small house; put in the garden with both ends open and used as a tunnel; transformed with the aid of a makeshift sail into a boat tackling Cape Horn in rough weather; a Jumbo Jet cockpit – just paint your box and glue on masses of dials made from tubes (the faithful toilet roll tube) or drawn with felt-tipped pens; a hospital, shop, office, home, or whatever make-believe game your child is playing.

There are two ways of making a car Add paper-plate wheels, cottage cheese-carton headlights and a paper-plate steering wheel to a painted box. Create luxury fittings with an old key, a number plate painted on the front and rear, and a bit of old carpet ...

Make your own puzzle If you find yourself with a lot of those little boxes from the cereal selections or a lot of old matchboxes you could make a box puzzle. Select a simple drawing, and divide it into matchbox-sized rectangles. Cut out the rectangles and glue them on to the matchboxes. You now have your puzzle pieces ready for your child to arrange and re-create the original drawing.

Box sculpture Get your child to paint with thick bright poster paints all over lots of different sized boxes, and then with children's glue stick them together in a shape. If you add string, the sculpture can be hung up.

A fantastic dragon made from milk cartons This is really brilliant-looking and very easy. Keep the containers from your daily milk (the biggest size is best) until you've got about ten of them. You'll also need an egg carton to cut up for the two eyes; white paper; Sellotape or glue; poster paint and paintbrushes; pipe cleaners or paper fasteners; glue and scissors.

Pull the milk carton completely open. From the top section cut away the two sides that are most creased up; repeat on each of your cartons. Cover the cartons with white paper and then give all but one to your child to paint (or decorate with things like lentils and silver-foil bottle caps).

While she is painting the dragon's body in a frenzy of lilac and red, you can concentrate on its head, which I have to admit is the trickiest bit. Cut off all the top folded section of the remaining carton. Starting at one corner cut a deep 'V' shape into the side of the carton to about half-way down and repeat on the other side to make it a deep mouth-shape from side-view. Glue the egg-carton eyes to the top of the head and hand over for painting on a fierce expression, preferably with many teeth!

To join the whole thing up overlap the top flaps of one carton on to the bottom flaps of the next one. In the centre of this overlap make two holes and thread a piece of pipe cleaner through, twisting the two ends of the cleaner together to allow for movement. If you haven't got pipe cleaners, use paper fasteners. Your child may want to add embellishments such as a tail made out of threaded macaroni or bottle tops or shells.

SAND PLAY

Buy washed sand and fill a purpose-built sandpit or an old paddling pool. It's a good idea to have two paddling pools because the one that you use for water play can then be used at night as a cover for the sand one, keeping out the rain and dead leaves. If your sandpit is starting to look dirty, it can easily be cleaned with baby bottle steriliser.

There are two things that toddlers shouldn't do in the sandpit: eat sand, or throw it, as it's horrible in your eyes.

Learning and playing Sand is hugely versatile. Toddlers can make patterns in it, build castles, pour it, press it, and load it in and out of a truck or indeed any size of container. Wet sand, although quite revolting to adult eyes, is good for tunnelling and patting, mixing up and moulding into shapes – and writing on. Now's the time to start teaching your child to write her name in the sand!

Encourage your child to draw pictures in smooth sand with a twig, or to create a town, and then play on the sand town with toy cars, or planes. Sand's great for playing Shops with – or playing Cooking.

IMAGINATIVE PLAY

From around two children will enjoy dressing up and will take part in quite complicated make-believe games. Peaches loves to spend time making up scenarios for herself and her dolls, attending to their every whim, or she pretends that she's baby bear. Later on she'll enjoy dressing up for these games.

One of my mother's most horrendous experiences was watching me swishing into one of her dinner parties at half-past ten at night, aged about four, wearing my mother's long red wig, and her diaphragm perched jauntily on the top of my head, saying to the bewildered guests, 'Hello, my name's Caraba of the East, how d'you like my hat?' Oddly enough, I found the wig last summer when I was pregnant and cleaning out drawers like a woman possessed, seminaked because of the excessive heat, and about ninety stone overweight. Thrilled with my find, wearing the wig slapped on squiffily and covering one eye, I ran outside to find my husband. Unfortunately, I ran straight into our verger (we live next door to the church) who calmly engaged me in ordinary conversation as though I was normally dressed.

Even if you and your toddler are not attending a toddler drama group – and quite a few places have these available – you'll find that by the time she's a little older you are suddenly the audience for mini plays, and the acting out of stories you have told her, or fantasies she has. Children find that fantasy games are useful for expressing fears.

One of the most interesting things about your child's make-believe play is how often it mirrors your behaviour. You'll notice her copying you and you'll wonder if you really do spend a lifetime chatting on your phone . . . If it's a tense time for you you'll notice she's tense or cross with her toys, and acts out her feelings with them. She'll accurately mimic mannerisms and even things that you say a lot during games of Mummies and Daddies. Fifi once told a

man she'd met in a swimming pool while playing with his little daughter that her parents didn't understand her; she was three and a half at the time. She informed him sadly that they spent all day kissing each other and had no time for swimming. This was said with a completely straight face and with me sitting right next to her. So don't worry if you find that your child's play acting isn't always entirely flattering.

Your dressing-up box Old high-heels, old jewellery, hairslides, feather boas, aprons, underwear, nighties, handbags, parasols, and wigs are all perfect. One thing I've noticed is that under-fives seem to have a special place in their hearts for any article of clothing *circa* 1972, and all of them were definitely members of The Sweet or T Rex in a past life. Anything Lurex or swirling puce Bri-Nylon with forty-eight-inch bell bottoms and a sequin trim will definitely be fought over. As well as discarded glitter and frills, it's a good idea to have a selection of hats. You can add feathers or flowers to give them that extra glamour!

Make your own hats The simple cone is easiest to start with – that can make anything from a witch's hat with a star and a moon on it to a dunce's cap. You can easily make crowns out of card and silver foil, and any toy 'professional' hats come in useful for acting games – policeman's helmet, nurse's hat, chef's hat etc. Scarves and tea towels are good for biblical epics!

For the cone hat, cut a circle of cardboard. The size of the circle will dictate the height of the cone so if you're making a hat for a Chinese coolie that'll be a smaller circle. Cut a slit from one edge right to the middle of the circle. Overlap the two sides until the hat fits your child's head, then tape securely. If you like, your child could then decorate the hat with stars, moons, flowers, glitter or ribbon. To keep the hat on securely you'll need to attach a piece of elastic to go under the chin.

For a paper-plate hat, all you need to do is punch a hole in each side of a paper plate and attach two strings (or pieces of ribbon) so that the plate can be worn. Your child will enjoy painting and decorating it.

False hair This needn't be a proper wig. You can plait tights to make an effective, rather Heidi-ish affair, or use raffia, string or wool.

Beards can be made from any of the above attached to a card board or fabric base, with string on the corners to tie around the child's head. Or you can simply stick cotton wool on to cardboard for a Santa-style moustache and beard.

Don't throw away your old make-up This will come in very useful when it comes to dressing up – as long as you keep a large tub of cleansing cream handy for afterwards. Follow this up with soap and water for thorough results. No one wants their child to go around looking like one of The Cure.

Make your own masks Just cut out some large, brightly coloured faces from glossy magazines and glue them on to cards, then attach to a lolly stick with Sellotape. Cut small holes for your child to see through. Alternatively, you could just make a nose, or a moustache, or eyes and eyebrows.

To make an animal mask, cut out a simple animal face and glue fur fabric or feathers from a duster on to the front. Add ties to each side, and have fun!

TIDYING UP AFTER PLAYING

I am one of those people who cannot sleep in a room if one of the curtains is slightly asymmetrical, so it bothers me a lot if at the end of the day of heavenly play the entire house looks exactly as though the SAS have spent several months training in the sitting-room.

If you are hoping that your husband or partner is going to return home to a sweet scene of heavenly domestic bliss rather than a scene of horror that stretches from one room to another, some way of preventing total chaos must be found.

Encourage your child to help you Even a two year old can put away a couple of things, and she will probably do so with gusto because two year olds love helping! And four and five year olds can have it explained to them why Mummy would like to remove some of the cold custard from the three-piece suite, even if they think it looks rather fetching.

Good storage It's much easier to keep everywhere tidy if you have a toy cupboard, or set of toy shelves, with a place or a box for everything. Alternatively if, like me, you feel this is simply too much to aim for, a very large basket that all the stuff on the floor can be flung into is the next best plan.

Stacking vegetable-racks and shoe-holders that can be fastened on to the backs of doors are good for smaller toys.

Chapter Two

Getting in Touch
with
Nature

Since I moved to the country I have embraced some of the great experiences of British life relatively unknown to the city dweller – like the cold. I run like Roger Bannister along the corridors between our bedroom and the loo, which is about four and a half miles away. I've discovered that if I don't run like the clappers I risk getting hypothermia and frostbite in the nether regions of my anatomy on the return journey.

But I've also opened a fête, and made crabapple jelly with my eldest daughter. The jelly turned out to have a consistency reminiscent of the effects of severe Dehli-belly, and both of us got scalded on the pan handle.

I realised how different life was in the country when I received a rather mysterious phone-call from a very grand lady asking if we'd like her ram to be sent over, because she'd heard we were the lucky owners of sixteen Jacob's sheep. Being the only Jacob's ram in the district, he was much in demand, hopping nimbly into the lady's ancient Bentley to be chauffeur-driven from farm to farm to perform his noble duties.

Although we haven't yet experienced an Agatha Christie-style body in our library I have had time to reacquaint myself with that great British tradition – the local amateur dramatic society. This was something I used to love when I was little, being brought up on the side of a mountain in Snowdonia – in our village amateur dramatics was one of the few things people did at night that didn't involve sheep.

Because my parents had been asked to leave the performance of *Kismet* when my mother laughed at the juvenile lead (the butcher's sixty-year-old wife in a pair of peach chiffonette pyjama bottoms tied around the ankles to make harem pants) the organisers decided to retaliate. They invited my dear mama to appear in their production of *Doctor in the House*. They planned to massacre this during the week of the sheepdog trials, thus ensuring packed houses and vast funds for the new roof on the village nissen hut. My mother's appearance in a shocking pink nylon négligé also guaranteed them a vast influx of manically bored Australian champion shearers.

On the big night my mother's great moment, when she was meant to be pertly lifted off the sofa by the Dirk Bogarde character (played by the postman, Alf Roberts), was destroyed. He slipped a disc mid-lift, flung her across the stage in a heap of nylon, and had to be carried off-stage on a door by three sheep shearers all waving to their mates and shouting 'Good on yer' at my mother.

The country conjures up visions of perfectly adjusted children with rosy cheeks, who don't watch *Friday the Thirteenth, Part 300* on the sofa with three skinhead six-year-old friends and a McDonald's, visions which make the average city-dwelling parent want to move there immediately and rid themselves of many worries. However, as I'm trying to be vaguely in touch with reality here, I'm aware that most of us will not be able to go and live in rose-strewn cottages in perfect villages, however heavenly it would be.

But there are lots of green activities your child can take part in at home. You and your child can get in touch with nature in the town as well as the countryside, and you'll be amazed at how therapeutic it can be if you're feeling harassed. Sometimes urban life is so fast-moving we forget how satisfying simply observing can be. Even in London there are trees, birds, and all sorts of little animals, insects and pondlife to be investigated. Encourage your child to keep a pet – and learn about animals. And a pet can be a playmate for a small child (as long as the creature isn't actually tortured), and someone to chat to if your child is lonely.

GREEN CHILDREN

I recently came across Fifi sitting at the kitchen table with her head in her hands. I thought she was worried about one of the major issues in her life like where she had put her ballet shoes or whether she could wangle watching *Polyanna* for the four hundredth time. I interrupted her only to be informed that she was worrying about the plight of the elephants and the dolphins, and the dirty sea at Herne Bay. Nowadays children are not only naturally curious about their environment but even small ones are aware of the threats to it. They realise that when they grow up they are the ones who will inherit the rubbish we have left behind. Your four or five year old may be a budding Jonathan Porritt but probably at the moment feels helpless. But there *are* things she can do to help, and there are many ways of becoming green on a small scale.

Recycle paper Most rubbish dumps have special skips that are just for paper, newspaper and cardboard. Keep this separately from your other rubbish so that it can be used again usefully. Encourage your child to conserve paper at home by using both sides of it. Waste paper can be used for drawing or painting on – little children won't mind where it comes from! Buy products made from recycled paper, like toilet tissue.

Save bottles Glass can be melted down and used again. All rubbish dumps and most public car-parks have bottle dumps. You have to take the tops off the bottles before you enjoy throwing them in the dump. All that smashing and crashing is a great release if you've had a horrible day.

Observe wildlife Stand at the window and look out, and you'll be amazed at how much is going on. When you are looking at birds, see how many different kinds you can identify. Do the same with insects, flowers and trees. Even if you're not keen on television, it is a good idea to encourage your green toddler to watch the nature programmes. You've got to convince her that she'd much rather watch a lesser-spotted weasel giving birth than the latest antics of Tom and Jerry.

Feed the birds Just putting a few slices of mouldy bread out is enough to encourage birds to come into the garden. Not only are you helping birds to survive in cold weather but helping your child to learn about them. Bacon rind or porridge oats are just as alluring as bread.

It's not that difficult to make your own bird table. All you need is a flat piece of wood attached to a high post out of the way of local cats. Try hanging those orange net bags filled with pellets, unpleasantly titled fat balls, off the table, and watch the acrobatics of birds like greenfinches. The Royal Society for the Protection of Birds publishes a leaflet about nesting boxes, and an excellent booklet, *Discover Garden Birds*.

The Royal Society for the Protection of Birds, The Lodge, Sandy, Bedfordshire SG19 2DL.

Make a pond If you do have a garden and you and your child are feeling really ambitious, you could make your own pond. This would encourage even more wildlife – not only birds, who will come to wash and drink, but also frogs, toads, and probably even worse things . . . Although building a pond sounds very daunting and expensive, it need not be if you use heavy plastic for the lining instead of fibreglass. You must remember to cover the pond with wire or plastic netting so that your child doesn't fall in, but the holes in the netting must allow frogs and toads access! The last thing you want to be doing is pushing a toad through a hole. To attract wildlife you need to plant reeds, water plants and a rockery around the edge of the pond. Your child will be able to watch tadpoles turning into frogs and discover fascinating creatures like snails and newts. If your child's anything like my daughter Peaches, she may attempt to eat the frogspawn, which is what I found Peaches doing last Saturday morning – much to my horror! Although she said they were delicious, eating frogspawn is not recommended!

Breed a butterfly This may sound bizarre, but it's perfectly possible to do at home. Caterpillar cages and butterfly eggs can be bought from the Butterfly Farm in Bath.

The Butterfly Farm, 6 Westwoods Box Road, Bathford, Bath BA1 7QE.

Join a club Encourage your child's interest in nature by getting her to join an organisation like Friends of the Earth. Most of these have a junior club or family membership.

Friends of the Earth, 26–28 Underwood Street, London N7 7JQ.

The London Wildlife Trust, 80 York Way, London N1 9AG.

Greenpeace, 30–31 Islington Green, London N1 8XE.

Wildlife Rescue, 29 Berkeley Drive, West Moseley, Surrey KT8 9RA.

The Woodland Trust, Autumn Park, Dysart Road, Grantham, Lincoln-shire NG31 6LL.

Visit a farm Many farms are now open to the public, especially during the summer. Don't forget city farms, of which there are now many all over the country.

The National Federation of City Farms, The Old Vicarage, 66 Fraser Street, Windmill Hill, Bedminster, Bristol BS3 4LY.

THINGS TO DO WITH NATURE'S BOUNTY

Leaf rubbings For this you will need some leaves (and it's best to use big ones, not titchy little ones); crayons; thin paper and tape. Place the leaves on the table, put the paper over the leaves, and then tape the paper down so that it can't move and get wrinkled up or ripped. Gently rub the crayon lengthways back and forth across the paper – the tracery of the veins, and the relief of your leaves will come through the paper.

Branch weavings You will need a branch that has at least four smaller branches shooting out from it; about three metres of coloured wool; and the items you've collected on your walk – long grasses, wheat, corn ears, feathers, sea shells, leaves.

Starting at the base of one small branch, loop the wool around to wrap it securely. Continue to wrap it to the next small branch, and all the way up so that you have a basis of slats of wool wrapped securely around each branch horizontally. Weave in your natural objects through the wool so that it holds them in place. Small children will wrap the wood around the branches in a very random way, but it will be enough to hold the trophies in place.

How to make a shell windchime Toddlers will love listening to the noise this makes, but personally I think this sort of very fey stuff is probably only acceptable to mothers living in areas where caftans and joss sticks are *de rigueur* and the entire Spinners back catalogue is sung every night at bedtime . . .

You'll need sea shells; strong coloured wool; an electric drill with a steel bit; and a branch or a piece of driftwood.

Drill a small hole into the end of all the shells you've found, then cut the wool to lengths that are long enough to hang down

decoratively but easy to tie on to the driftwood. Tie a shell on one end of the wool, and then tie the other end on to the wood. Have lots of shells on one string of wool, and only a few on another, and so on, and space them all fairly close to one another on the branch, so they knock together once the driftwood is hung up and the wind blows them gently.

Shell jewellery Having gone to the trouble of drilling holes in your shells, you could use some of them to make jewellery. Thread the shells, along with painted macaroni, or beads, or even buttons, on to elastic to make necklaces and bracelets . . .

Fish printing This is completely brilliant even though it sounds rather strange – and as long as you thoroughly wash the fish afterwards you can still eat it for your tea.

The best fish for fish printing are big flat fish with large scales. You also need powder paints; paintbrush; blotting paper and newspaper.

Lay your catch (even if you caught it at Waitrose) on to the newspaper, dry it and then paint it. Now, taking great care, put the blotting paper on the fish. Your child should have dry hands and hold the fish completely flat as she rubs it over the paper. When the paper's been lifted off and allowed to dry there will be a print of your fish, scales, eyes, and all!

Wood collages Any bits of wood you may have collected together, even shavings, twigs, or bits of bark, can be stuck on to a large sheet of paper with PVA glue and made into a design. Nuts, pine needles, pebbles – even sand – can be glued on too.

A bedroom garden Why not make a little model garden together. You'll need some casting plaster, which can be bought cheaply at a DIY shop; flowers; twigs; small branches; pine cones; even small rocks from your walk in the park or countryside . . .

Spread the plaster on the bottom of an old plate, or a paper plate, and stick all the objects in to make a pretty arrangement. We once made a really tiny one from a section of an eggbox with a daisy as a tree.

THE FUN DON'T STOP

Pressing flowers All you do is put the flowers between two sheets of paper inside a heavy book, and put that in between all your other books on the shelf so that the book is held firmly shut. Once the flowers are pressed they'll be *very* delicate – but you'll be able to make pictures, book marks (covered in see-through vinyl covering), and cards or calendars with them.

Stone painting For this you'll need some smooth, large pebbles; some clear gloss paint or varnish; and some powder paints and paintbrushes.

On to the pebble paint a pattern, or an animal, or even a scene of the place where you collected the pebbles, and then varnish it to a glossy shine so that the picture is protected. This is effective on a tiny pebble or on a massive lump of rock, and you can do lots of them and put them all around the flower-beds in the garden, on either side of the front door, or make a large one into a door-stop.

GARDENING MAGIC

As will be clear from the frogspawn saga, our family is not one to be afraid of eating something revolting. My husband ate a slug as a child, and Peaches relished an earwig in our garden last summer whilst helping the gardener with a bit of potting which he would undoubtedly have finished in half the time without her help.

Gardening can be performed without the aid of a garden. Aim small to begin with: for example, any child enjoys writing her name in seeds on blotting paper and then watching the seeds sprout over the next few days. A lot of parents are put off growing things with a child because they imagine she might be bored, but in fact there are lots of plants that grow quickly and reward with blossoms and blooms in a very short time. You can have fun with pot plants and window boxes and all sorts of imaginative containers. A friend of mine bought a step-shaped shelving unit for her tiny balcony, and completely covered the unit with chamber pots filled with Busy Lizzies and tiny vegetables and herbs...

If you live in the country you may be able to let your child have her own patch of garden so that she can plant a profusion of mismatched but riotously coloured flowers.

Children who learn about gardening will understand that carrots come out of the ground, and not from plastic containers. I'm still *amazed* whenever I'm in America by the fact that no American realises that milk comes from a cow, and they all think that cream is something you whip up from a powder in the Moulinex.

There's always the chance that things will go wrong, so it's a good idea to have a gardening book at hand – or better still a friend who knows something about it. But if you and your child stick to simple projects, you shouldn't have any trouble!

Growing from seed Planting seeds with your child is pleasant for you both, and need not take up lots of space. Not only will your child be able to watch her plant slowly growing (or possibly dying) but she will also be able to enjoy the scent if you choose the right plants. Night-scented stocks, lavender and honeysuckle are wonderful. Plants that give off scent at night also encourage moths. Or you might choose to plant flowering herbs like chives or thyme, both of which will attract bees and butterflies to your windowsills and paths. Children love sunflowers. They're very easy to grow and look so impressive, if not ideal for the kitchen table. Encourage small birds and animals to your garden by planting a hedge, like the ones that used to be everywhere when I was little, made of hawthorn, or beech.

To plant seeds you will need a seed tray and a bag of compost. Sprinkle the seeds over the compost and then cover them with a light layer of soil. Water the seeds very gently – don't flood them into a sodden mass. Then tie a plastic bag over the whole of the tray and put it into a warm, dark place. We put ours under the sink which is next to the boiler, and had marvellous flowers later in the year. As soon as the shoots begin to appear, take the box out of the bag and put it in a warm, light place, but not in direct sunlight. Keep the seedlings damp, and as soon as they have at least six leaves they are ready to be replanted 5 cm apart in a new tray so that they have room for expansion. The next move will be into the garden or window box.

Growing from bulbs This is very satisfying, and bulbs cost a pocket-money amount. Why not try snowdrops, daffodils, bluebells, crocuses, tulips or hyacinths. They should be planted in the autumn and you'll need a pot; gravel; and compost. Half-fill your pot with the compost and put the bulbs gently on the top with their pointed ends upright. Plant them close together, then cover them up with compost and water them. Put them in a cool dark place for a couple of months. Don't forget to keep the soil damp during this time. When the little buds are about 5 cm in size put the pots in a light but still cool place and water them regularly. As they get taller you must move them somewhere warmer. Cut off the dead heads when they have finished flowering. Plant them outside for next year. Hyacinth bulbs can be started off in water. Fill a special bulb jar with water to just below the bulb and then put it into a dark place until the roots are about 10 cm long.

Houseplants If you are living in a confined space and don't have access to large window ledges or a balcony, let alone a garden, fear not, you can still cultivate glorious houseplants. You could contemplate anything from an African violet to a drooping, chiffonlike asparagus or a glamorous azalea.

You'll need compost; a sponge; plant food; sticks; a watering can; a little plastic mister and some string. When you buy the plant find out what its needs are. All plants have definite personalities (rather like opera singers, I've discovered). You should know what amount of light and warmth your plant requires before you bring it to its new home. No plant likes draughts, and all plants need watering when dry. During the summer months you should step up the watering. Try standing the plant on a saucer of water, so it can suck the water up that way. To prove to your child that a plant takes in water, just stick a white carnation into a bottle of inky water and watch the carnation turn blue.

Remember that in spring and summer the plants will grow a lot faster, and that the way to make them even bushier is to nip off the growing tips of the new shoots.

Trees To grow a tree all you need is a pot and saucer; compost; some plastic bags; pebbles; and a gardening fork (not the family silver). In ten years your child will have a beautiful tree thronging with nests and the tree will probably have moved the garage three feet to the left! Trees can be grown from conkers, ash seeds, pine cones, beech nuts, acorns, or even holly berries. You could also try planting fruit pips. You must plant each seed separately in a small pot, water it thoroughly and then tie a plastic bag over the pot to keep the soil damp. Put your pots on a sunny windowsill. You have to wait quite a long time for any action – about two months, I'm afraid – but when the seedling does appear, whip off the plastic bag and water your baby tree each week. When autumn comes, plant the tree outside remembering not to put it too near your own or anyone else's house, as it might develop huge, tentacle-like roots and rip up the outside toilet. Plant each of your baby trees with a strong stick next to it; fill the hole with soil and tie the tree to the stick so that it doesn't topple over in a heap. Water and wait!

Wild flowers If you have enough space (and your child is a budding romantic) you might like to create a patch of old-fashioned wild flowers. One of the great tragedies of modern life is that since the beginning of the century more than twenty species of British wild flowers have been lost for ever. You can grow wild flowers in a window box, too, and the seeds are available from any garden centre. The Royal Society for Nature Conservation publishes a very good leaflet on wild flower gardening. Buddleia, daisies, candy tufts, and sweet williams are particularly good at encouraging butterflies.

The Royal Society for Nature Conservation, Vigilant Ho, 120 Wilton Road, London SW1V 1JZ

Herbs You can buy herbs as plants from most garden centres or grow them from seed. They'll grow indoors or out, but they must be well drained. If you're growing them in a pot make sure you put pebbles in the bottom.

An annual like parsley is best grown from a small plant, unless you have perfectly green fingers. Keep parsley in the shade and water it frequently. Or try mint, which is not only a delicious addition to your cooking but which has the added bonus of attracting bees to the flowers. Once you have grown some thyme, why not try drying it by hanging the bunches upside down for a deeply rustic look in your kitchen and a delicious smell. A friend did this with large bunches of garlic and cinnamon sticks all tied up with tartan ribbons. Rosemary is another popular herb, it grows very tall and looks marvellous. Chives need a lot of watering but in return grow pretty little pink flowers. You shouldn't let your herbs flower if you're going to use them for cooking, though. Just nip off the flower buds and the herb leaves will get thicker and be ready for consumption.

Broad beans You'll need dried beans; some sheets of kitchen paper; and a glass jar. Roll up about six sheets of paper and put them into the jar, then push the beans between the paper and the glass. Pour water into the jar to moisten the paper and put the jar in a warm place. Check it every day and watch the beans swell up before they start to split and grow shoots. Once the plant is about 15 cm in size it's time to transfer it into a bigger plant pot with a hole in the bottom. Keep up the watering and make sure the plant gets plenty of light.

Avocados and sweet potatoes Like the hyacinth bulb, these can be grown in water. Balance the avocado stone or sweet potato (with the aid of toothpicks) over a large bottle of water. With any luck it will start to shoot, and you should then transfer the little plant to a pot.

Tomatoes It is a well-known fact that food you've managed to grow yourself tastes a million times better than shop-bought food, and it is also a very good way of persuading toddlers to eat vegetables which otherwise they would spit across the table at high velocity.

Tomatoes can be grown either from a seed, or from a small plant, and will grow indoors or outdoors as long as you put them in a sunny sheltered place. To plant the tomato plant you need to fill a *big* plant pot (at least 25 cm across) with compost, put a cane in it and dig a small hole. Put in the plant and fill in the pot with more compost. Press it down firmly around your little seedling and water. Put the plant in a warm, sunny spot and water it often, taking care to water the roots and not the leaves. Tie the plant loosely to a long cane when it starts to get too tall to support itself, and when it finally flowers you'll need to shake it gently each day so that the pollen gets distributed.

When there are four bunches of tomatoes (HURRAH!) on the plant, pinch off the topmost shoot. Pick the tomatoes when they're bright red, taking care to leave the stalk on the plant.

Runner beans Beans are great to grow because you don't need a garden. They'll happily grow in a pot on a balcony or a small patio.

The first thing to do is fill a very large, bucket-sized pot with compost – stick three very tall canes in, and tie them up at the top to make a sort of pyramid shape. Plant a seed next to each of these sticks – the shoots will appear in about three weeks. As they continue to grow, carefully wind them around the sticks, and water the potting compost to keep it nice and damp. When the little bean flowers appear, spray them with water, as this helps further pods to appear. Finally, pick your beans when they are young, like they say in the adverts on TV. A ready-to-pick bean is around 10 cm long and breaks into two easily.

Potatoes Look in the mouldy depths of your vegetable rack and find a sprouting potato, and leave it on a sunny windowsill until the shoots are 2 cm long. Leave the two best-looking shoots and rub all the rest off, then put stones into the bottom of a 25 cm pot and half-fill it with potting compost. Plant your potato so that the shoots are at the top, and water it. A month later more green shoots should appear; cover these with yet more potting compost, and keep on doing this until your bucket is full to the top with compost.

Later on, you'll find that your potato plant will flower. Once the flowers die, don't water the plant, as the potatoes will rot if they get sodden. Instead, wait until the plant actually dies, then tip everything out on to a plastic bin liner laid on the floor and count how many potatoes you've grown together!

A cress head Break an empty eggshell in half and put a little blotting paper into the bottom of each half. Dampen the blotting paper and sprinkle it with cress seeds. In just a few days the cress will grow and look like hair. Draw a little face on each shell-half in felt-tipped pen.

Cress hands and feet A variation on the theme of the cress head is to plant the cress in a plaster cast of your child's hand or feet. You can buy casting powder at most hardware shops. A little poster paint will brighten it up.

ANIMAL FUN

If there was one event that crystallised in my mind the sheer horror of being a mum – and if we are being honest we must all occasionally face it – it was an incident the other day involving our esteemed family pet Growler, who is a very overweight Yorkshire terrier, and bears a startling resemblance to the family, except that he has a tail. I staggered out of bed after a hard night's snoring and breast-feeding (which I have a unique ability to do simultaneously) to go downstairs and give Growler his morning portion of soya dog-diet food. He is currently on the canine equivalent of the F-plan Diet, or misery-plan diet as my husband calls it ... So far the diet has done little for his girth because he spends his every waking moment trying to get outside so that he can ransack our neighbours' dustbins for remnants of *pâté de foie gras* or Chum or anything. This time, his ransacking was having dire results, as I was soon to find out. Naked, I reached the bottom of the stairs, and skidded at astonishingly high speed on a streak of dog pooh several feet long, induced no doubt by excessive scavenging for old food. Splattered, I hit the front door with my cheeks pulled in like Buzz Aldrin during take-off and wondered for the millionth time why children *love pets* so much.

Apart from giving your child something to lavish love on and boss around (so giving any younger brother or sister a break), and teaching your child about animal behaviour, pets can also encourage a sense of responsibility. However, I've found that even an eight year old will balk at dishing out dog food, and forget the water bowl unless reminded – and no one likes combing out long-haired pets.

Which pet Your choice of pet is important, not only for the obvious reason that it has to be cute and adorable, but also because it has to fit easily into your family life. The size of your home, whether or not you have a garden, how much energy you're prepared to put into looking after the animal, will all have to be taken into consideration. Don't choose a dog like Growler who (you won't be surprised to hear) turned out to be impossible to train. My husband bought him for me as a cure for post-natal depression after I'd had Fifi. After a year Growler was still incapable of walking down the street without getting into trouble and ended up having to travel everywhere in the pram with the baby!

Reptiles, like terrapins and tortoises, are 'low-maintenance' pets, but not really the sort of creatures you want to sit looking lovingly at for hours on end as you caress the scales on their fourteen chins.

There are some breeds of dogs that are simply not safe around children, despite what their wily breeders may claim. So Rottweilers, Alsatians and pit bull terriers can all be forgotten. Even some breeds of smaller dogs are not temperamentally suited to endless tail-pulling and games. My granny had a collie that had a nervous breakdown after I went to stay with her at the age of six. Shortly after I left the two of them were walking down a steep staircase when the collie nipped my granny viciously on the behind, whereupon she swiftly turned and bit the end of its tail off. This story is still repeated at family dinner parties. So, when buying a dog, it's a good idea to call your vet and get his recommendations for a good, child-centred breed!

Fish in a bowl need very little of your time, unlike their more glamorous tropical counterparts, but like reptiles they're part of the no-cuddle syndrome.

Parrots pooh everywhere, eat all the flower arrangements and occasionally nip – but can be taught to say interesting things and do look gorgeous.

Rabbits are appealing to children, but I find their allure wears a bit thin. After having them for a month or so, you discover they haven't got the most interesting personalities in the animal kingdom, and usually have to be forced to co-operate when it comes to cuddles, which irritates a toddler with love gushing from her every pore!

The idea of keeping a pony may seem wildly extravagant but if you live in the country with a great deal of space it's something worth considering. Peaches and Fifi learnt to ride at the age of two

and since then a fine time has been had by all at gymkhanas, on pony treks and on ordinary rides. A passionate interest in riding might also stave off the evil day of the under-ten disco scene as in her enthusiasm your daughter tramps around at dawn mucking out.

Pets and health hazards Never allow an animal to lick your child's mouth, and make sure you have cats and dogs wormed regularly. Worm eggs are passed in bowel motions, and can survive in earth or dust for a long time. It is estimated that two children a week in this country go blind as a result of contact with worm eggs. Small children should never be allowed near a litter tray.

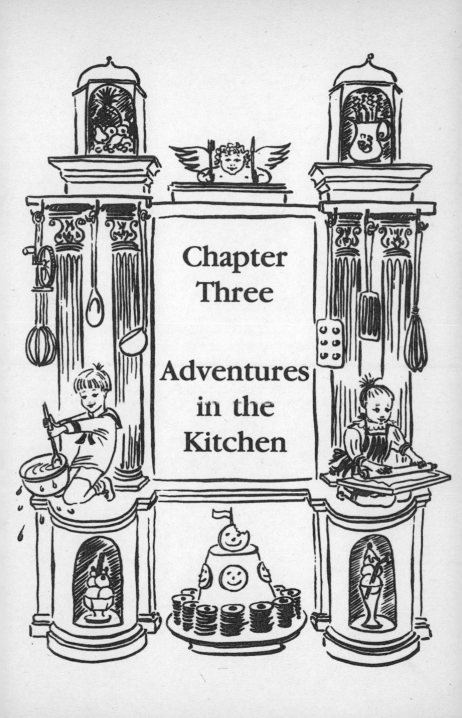

Chapter
Three

Adventures
in the
Kitchen

This morning I lunged out of bed, thinking this is it, today I feel filled with the strength to start my diet and resist the temptation to have three eggs, fried bread and a mountain of toast in order to have the strength to make it to lunchtime ... Since I had my third baby it has been a constant source of amazement to me that month by month I have managed to shift absolutely nil weight. The first three stone came off fairly soon after the birth, but I'm left with two of the rather impressive five stone I managed to put on during the pregnancy! And needless to say there are many mixed emotions from those near and dear to me: my husband remains furiously supportive and resolutely pretends he hasn't noticed any change at all, but at the same time he actually fights with my hand if he sees it near chocolate, cream, or for some reason salad dressing. My friends either commiserate or chortle gleefully, the laughter of those less noble beings who are delighted you don't measure 20-20-20 any more and hope that you end up posing for the 'before' pictures on slimming adverts, and never wear Pucci leggings again as a punishment for your past life as a thin person.

Anyway, there I was this morning, racing downstairs to the bathroom scales, acting as though they looked like Nicholas Cage and I couldn't wait to jump on them. Once I got there I looked down at the swinging arm pointing at a three-figure poundage, and stopped dead. 'This is worse than anticipated,' I panted. 'After the run downstairs, I'm already peckish.' I wondered whether I should do my usual trick, which is to stand on the scales in the bathtub. On our machine this automatically makes you lose two stone. If that fails there's a knob on the underneath that you can adjust so that you suddenly weigh about as much as Wayne Sleep's tights.

I was convinced there must have been some mistake – carefully I removed my ear-rings, a corn plaster and my hair band, and looked behind me in case one of the children was standing surreptitiously on the scales encouraging my plateau stage. (I am one of the few would-be post-pregnancy dieters who is at her plateau stage before she's started the diet . . .)

It was then that I decided I wanted to be unhappy. Yes, I admit it, the gay Joyce Grenfell of Kent decided to wholeheartedly torture herself by standing on the edge of the bath. In our house, where there are no full-length mirrors, this is the only way that one can get a full-length view of the real horrors eddying around knicker level. So there I was, precariously balanced on the soap dish, corns throbbing, hair flapping, weight actually soaring by the minute, gazing in horror at what had been allowed to occur because I'm so lazy and I love eating with every member of the family including the dog . . .

The biggest problem with trying to diet with kids around is that they eat lots of delicious things in front of you, most of which are fattening, I've noticed. And when you're on the way to the park you can't help but suddenly notice how much Pizza Hut is now spending on advertising.

What I have attempted to do is put all the family on a healthy-eating regime, which I think they'll probably write about in later life in a sort of 'Mommy Dearest' book: *Our mother suddenly decided we were all going to eat cottage cheese and pineapple chunks for tea when the weather was COLD and every day ad infinitum!* I, on the other hand, am taking up Lean Cuisines. Personally, I suspect that there are more calories in the boxes they come in: to me the helping looks so small on the plate that, even pretending it's *nouvelle*-style, I wonder whether I shouldn't have the box with some prawn cocktail sauce on it as a starter. My husband loves them but he has three at once.

Apart from making you totally obsessed with when you're going to eat next, dieting makes you long to watch what everyone else is eating, and help them cook it too – even if you're not going to eat it you can fondle that soufflé together. Cooking with children takes a great deal longer than zipping into the kitchen and doing it on your own, but it is a satisfying activity for you both, and in my case at the moment my only contact with a chocolate-covered rice crispie . . .

One of the things that I was astonished to discover about Peaches was her passionate desire to help with the washing up. It was this that alerted me to future possibilities, maybe she would not be averse to hoovering, kitchen-floor polishing, perhaps even a course in foot massage ... At the moment, though, her great interest lies in the kitchen. She watches me preparing food and notices two things: I make a massive amount of mess and no one tells me off, and the results (with a bit of luck) are edible. Cooking's a grown-up activity she'd definitely like to discover more about.

Even babies like watching food being prepared, and joining in by playing with vegetables or anything else you can spare for some play cooking. Once your baby is big enough to be fascinated by putting small things into bigger containers you could give her a large bowl of pasta shapes and an empty pile of mini cereal boxes for her to fill to her heart's content.

Of course all of this is just delaying the moment when she wants to really *assist*! This is also the moment when cooking starts to take at least fourteen times as long and probably several weeks to get bits of guacamole off the ceiling.

It's wise to follow a few guidelines before you start to cook with your child. Never let her touch the cooker, and turn all the pan handles inwards. Teach her from the word go to use a *blunt* knife only, and never leave her alone with it. Make sure she washes her hands before she starts, otherwise you'll end up with jam tarts flavoured with something disgusting. Clear up any spills on kitchen floors to prevent anyone slipping and falling over, and *never leave a child unsupervised for one second*.

RECIPES FOR TINY TOTS

Extremely young children can't really cook as such, but still like the feeling of control they get from arranging food to their liking and doing plenty of mixing up!

Puddings and Dips

A good starting point is powdered instant pudding which you just add to milk. Let your child mix furiously until she has made something she can eat, and she'll enjoy decorating the pudding with a few halves of glacé cherries.

A lot of supermarkets sell dips in packets – ranging from simple cheese ones to all sorts of Mexican types which would probably blow the average toddler's nappy to Huddersfield. Like puddings, dips are easy for a toddler to mix up, and then you can provide a plate of crisps or small strips of cut-up vegetables for her to dip into her creation. A small dish of dip and crudités will keep a hungry toddler happily occupied for some time while you get on with the serious (loathsome) peeling . . .

Celery and Cheese Sticks

Cut up a long celery stick into one-inch-long chunks and spread each one with a little dab of cream cheese. Give your budding Jean-Pierre Higginbottom a dish of raisins, slices of apple, halves of grapes to stick into the cheese, and then eat up.

Bananas and Ice-cream

Slice up a largish banana and give it to your child along with a small dish of ice-cream and some raspberry-ripple sauce. She can then arrange it all into a mini banana split. Or use honey for the sauce, and add chopped-up dried fruits, nuts, or fresh fruits if you prefer.

Creative Savouries

Baked potatoes can be decorated with tiny slices of cheese and tomato (once the potatoes have been allowed to cool). With a little help from you, your child could make a potato into a boat – make sails out of lettuce and a toothpick.

Small, round pizzas can be made into mouse, cat or dog faces by arranging black olives, cheese strips and tomato circles on them and then toasting them lightly under the grill.

Food Sculptures

toothpicks
apples, oranges or any other fruit that your child enjoys
carrots, cucumbers, potatoes
sultanas
any soft sweets
pipe cleaners
marshmallows
olives, lettuce, parsley, cress

It's a good idea to slightly cook the vegetables so that it's easy to stick the bits and pieces on toothpicks without stabbing yourself. Use the different trimmings to make the vegetables into faces, with glasses made out of the pipe cleaners, hair made out of parsley or shredded lettuce leaves. Olives make good eyes, and carrot slices make sticking out ears. Alternatively, use the fruit as a base, and stick on sweets and sultanas.

Everyone knows that children seem to have a natural aversion to all things green and edible, but they can sometimes be persuaded to eat them if they've had a hand in preparing their salad and making it look astonishing. A clown face can be easily created on a large plate – make hair from lettuce leaves, ears from cucumber slices, the face itself, from smoothly mashed potatoes, and the eyes from slices of hard boiled egg and olives or black grapes. Cress eyebrows, a tomato nose and mouth and red cheeks, and a carrot bow tie can all be conjured up out of the vegetable basket.

Rice Crispie Figures

rice crispies
2 oz (50 g) butter or margarine
8 oz (225 g) marshmallows
currants, glacé cherries
pipe cleaners

Melt the butter on a medium heat in a saucepan, add the marshmallows and continue to stir until they have melted. Add enough rice crispies to make a stiff consistency. Remove from the heat.

Lay out a sheet of foil or greaseproof paper (the foil needs to be lightly greased so that the mixture doesn't stick to it). Then scoop out several large spoonfuls from the saucepan. With a little butter on the hands, roll the warm mixture into shapes – caterpillars made out of a series of balls are easy, or little men and women with eyes and buttons made from the cherries.

Make legs and antennae for the creatures out of pipe cleaners.

You can also make rice crispie cakes with 8 oz (225 g) melted chocolate instead of the marshmallows and simply spoon the mixture into paper cake cases.

Marzipan Fruits and Animals

8 oz (225g) marzipan
food colouring
whole cloves

Break the marzipan into five balls and put each ball into a separate bowl. Add a few drops of food colouring and work all the colouring into the marzipan with your hands. Make mini watermelons, peaches, oranges, plums, bananas, apples and strawberries using the cloves as stalks. Alternatively you might want to attempt a few pink elephants, or bright-green frogs with long pink or red tongues flicking out. Sit the frogs on marzipan lily pads!

Fruit and Nut Chocolates

8 oz (225 g) chocolate
2 oz (50 g) chopped nuts
2 oz (50 g) sultanas
2 oz (50 g) glacé cherries
1 teaspoon vegetable oil

You'll have to melt the chocolate either over hot water or in the microwave for about a minute before you add the oil and mix it in to a smooth consistency. Now add all the other ingredients and spoon the mixture into little paper cases. Put them into the fridge to set.

Icing Sculptures

1 lb 2 oz (500 g) icing sugar
4 large egg whites
1 teaspoon lemon juice
food colouring
smarties
chocolate fingers
pipe cleaners

Have the egg whites waiting at room temperature while you sift the icing sugar, then beat the egg whites gently in a bowl with a wooden spoon, adding the sugar a teaspoon at a time, continuing to beat well after each addition. Once your icing sugar has reached the correct consistency add the lemon juice for quick drying, and beat this really well!

If you have icing sugar left over you can seal it in an airtight container in the freezer and it will keep fresh for about a week.

With the addition of one or two smarties and chocolate fingers and a little food colouring, plus a few pipe cleaners to hold things together, you can make successful faces, cars, animals and farmyard scenes.

RECIPES FOR OLDER PRE-SCHOOLERS

A four year old will with your assistance be able to tackle cooked treats (with you in charge of the cooker). She will enjoy cooking things that are shaped like something else or wildly overdecorated.

A Basic Recipe for a Biscuit

Biscuits that you make from this mix can be cut into innumerable shapes: ducks, people, pigs, circles, stars, moons, butterflies, dogs, cats, trees, hearts, ponies. These are all easily made with either a knife, the hands, or a cutter. Your child will enjoy icing and decorating the biscuits. Remember to have a small box in your kitchen ready for these sessions containing silver balls, chocolate drops, smarties, hundreds and thousands, vermicelli – in fact, anything that will make good eyes, noses, pretty patterns. You can substitute other flavourings for the cinnamon in the biscuit mix – a little grated orange or lemon peel, grated-up chocolate, ground ginger, 2 oz (50 g) dried fruit or nuts. To make a savoury biscuit, leave out the sugar and put in 2 oz (50 g) grated cheese, and 2 oz (50 g) chopped-up, cooked sausage.

3 oz (75 g) butter
1 level tablespoon baking powder
1 level dessertspoon cinnamon
2 oz (50 g) golden syrup
4 oz (110 g) soft brown sugar
10 oz (275 g) plain flour
1 egg

For the icing
4 oz (110 g) icing sugar
1 tablespoon hot water

Pre-heat the oven to gas mark 3, 325°F (170°C).

Put the flour and cinnamon into a big mixing bowl and add your sugar, then add the butter, cut up into little bits, and rub everything together until it's in little lumps. In a separate bowl, beat the egg gently with a fork and add the golden syrup. Pour into the first mixing bowl and knead the mixture into a big ball of dough.

Put the dough into a plastic bag and leave it in the fridge for about half an hour: this makes it much easier to roll out. Sprinkle the table with some flour and roll out the dough so that it's about a quarter of an inch thick. It's now ready to shape into biscuits.

To make the icing for your biscuits, sift the icing sugar into a bowl. Add the water, a little at a time, until you have a smooth substance that's ready to spread. Don't try to ice the biscuits when they are hot from the oven, because the icing will just slide straight off again. Decorate to your heart's delight!

Cheesy Bread Bears

This recipe was a huge hit when we tried it at home. To make a family of three bears, you will have to double the ingredients.

½ sachet dried yeast (quick action type)
1 dessertspoon sunflower oil
10 fl oz (275 ml) warm water
large pinch of salt
12 oz (350 g) strong white flour
caraway, sesame or poppy seeds
sultanas
grated cheese

Pre-heat the oven to gas mark 8, 450°F (230°C).

Put the flour, yeast, and salt into a big mixing bowl, and add to it

the oil and water. Then mix everything together to make a firm dough, adding more water if the dough seems too stiff and dry. Put it on to a well-floured surface and knead for five minutes. Push your hands into it and then turn it over. Your child will probably be very efficient at pummelling the dough thoroughly! Shape the dough into bear-shapes, sticking the limbs together (and the noses on to the faces!) with a little egg, if necessary. After you've left them in a warm place and they've doubled in size, decorate them with sesame, caraway or poppy seeds and sultanas, and sprinkle with the grated cheese. Bake them for fifteen to twenty minutes. They are ready when they sound hollow when tapped underneath.

Teddy Bear Biscuits

2 oz (50 g) self-raising flour
2 oz (50 g) plain wholemeal flour
1 teaspoon ground cinnamon
½ teaspoon ground ginger
2 oz (50 g) light brown sugar
3 teaspoons runny honey
2 oz margarine

Pre-heat the oven to gas mark 6, 400°F (200°C).

Blend the flour and spice together, then add the margarine and sugar until well mixed in. Add the honey and knead to a firm dough. Shape into bears using either a cutter or a *blunt* knife. Transfer to a lightly greased baking sheet and bake for about eight minutes or until golden brown.

A Perfect Sponge

Although I am a great believer in children understanding where food comes from, that vegetables grow and don't come out of the can or freezer, when it comes to cakes I'm a firm devotee of the American cake mixes you can buy in most supermarkets (milk chocolate flavour especially). The mixes result in such massive,

69

wobbling, towering edifices of flamboyant delicious sponge that they cannot be faulted by any member of your family, and your child will feel so proud of her efforts. They are great fun to make with a child as they need strenuous stirring, which I enjoy too, and which I imagine will eventually increase my bust size by several feet.

Once your cake has cooled the two of you can decide what would be the most attractive type of decoration for it, which is half the fun again!

Pastry Delights

You might like to try making pastry with your child (not necessarily from scratch, although that's part of the fun, and the mess). Rolling out frozen ready-made pastry is always a hit. Pastry tarts can be filled with tinned peach halves and glazed over with melted-down jam, or simply filled with cold jam. Beware if you're heating jam – it gets astonishingly hot!

Banana Bread

6 oz (175 g) self-raising flour
2 oz (50 g) sugar
1 dessertspoon golden syrup
1 very large banana, mashed
1 egg
milk

Pre-heat the oven to gas mark 3, 325°F (170°C).

Mix everything up together in the bowl to make a smoothish, slightly runny paste and put it into a well-greased baking dish. Bake in the oven for twenty-five minutes, or until the bread looks solid. You may find that sticking a knife in is not the best test as this bread should be slightly moist when cooked. It is almost better eaten the next day, although it's delicious eaten hot with a glass of milk.

Syrupy Flapjacks

4 oz (110 g) butter
1 oz (25 g) sugar
2 teaspoons golden syrup
8 oz (225 g) rolled oats
½ level teaspoon salt

Pre-heat the oven to gas mark 4, 350°F (180°C).

Grease an eight-by-ten-inch baking tin. Melt the sugar, butter and syrup together over a low heat, then thoroughly mix in the oats and salt. Pour into the tin and bake for ten to twelve minutes. When the flapjack is firm, cut into slices in the tin. Don't turn it out until it's completely cold or it will crumble.

SUGARLESS TREATS

Having both made yourselves feel thoroughly ill eating sugary delights you may wish to turn your talents to some sugarless treats...

Sugarless Date Fudge

vanilla essence
4 oz (110 g) roughly chopped stoned dates
5 fl oz (150 ml) evaporated milk
1 oz (25 g) finely chopped nuts
1 oz (25 g) desiccated coconut or ground almonds

Over a low heat bring the dates and milk to the boil and then simmer for five minutes; stir so that the mixture doesn't stick. Remove the pan from the heat and add the vanilla essence and the chopped nuts. Leave the mixture to cool and then shape it into balls. Roll the balls in the coconut or almonds and put them into little paper cases.

Fruit Balls

2 oz (50 g) stoned dates
1 oz (25 g) raisins
4 oz (110 g) crunchy peanut butter
2 teaspoons carob powder
2 oz (50 g) sugarless apple juice concentrate

In a food processer blend the dates and raisins until they form a smooth paste, then (by hand) mix them with the other ingredients.

Put this mixture into an icing bag and pipe it into little paper cases. Sprinkle with carob powder.

If you think that piping is a bit ambitious for your child you can just roll the mixture into balls, then roll the balls in the carob powder.

Seed Squares

5 fl oz (150 ml) apple and apricot concentrate
1 oz (25 g) sunflower seeds
1 oz (25 g) sesame seeds

Lightly grease an eight-inch square baking tin. In a heavy-bottomed pan bring the concentrate to the boil, then simmer for three to five minutes. Test this syrup by placing a drop of it in a saucer of cold water – if it forms a stiff ball it's ready for action. Plunge the bottom of the pan into cold water and fling in all the seeds. Stir to make sure the seeds have sunk in, and pour the mixture into the tin, spreading it evenly with a greased spoon and then leaving to set before cutting into squares.

No Sugar Toffee Apples

3 medium sized apples, washed and dried
4 oz (110 g) clear honey
¼ teaspoon cream of tartar

Push a lolly stick very firmly into each apple. In a heavy-bottomed pan bring the honey to the boil, add the cream of tartar and then simmer gently for three to five minutes. Test the honey by dropping a little of it into a saucer of cold water; if it forms a ball it's ready. Place the base of the pan in cold water and then spoon the 'toffee' very very quickly over each apple so that it's covered. Leave the apples to set on well-greased paper.

Peach Jelly

8 oz (225 g) tinned peach slices in juice
¼ oz (5 g) powdered gelatine
2 teaspoons orange juice or water

Drain the peaches (keep the juice) and chop them up. Put into two small containers. Sprinkle the gelatine over the orange juice or water and melt it over a bowl of hot water taking care to stir it all the time. Next add 7 fl oz (200 ml) peach juice to the melted gelatine and stir well. Pour into the fruit in the little containers. Chill in the fridge until set and ready for tea.

RECIPES TO LURE THE FADDY EATER

If your child is fussy and you've had difficulties with her eating, try milkshakes. A really nutritious one is a sort of meal in a glass; those that I've included here are also suitable for vegans or children with an allergy to dairy produce. They are simplicity itself for your child to make.

Soya Milk Shake

10 fl oz (275 ml) soya milk
2 teaspoons apple and strawberry juice concentrate

With an electric whisk, beat up the milk and juice until really thick and foamy; serve in a long glass.

Banana Milkshake

2 oz (50 g) stoned dates
10 fl oz (275 ml) milk
¼ teaspoon wheatgerm
1 very large banana

Place the dates in a saucepan with half the milk and then bring to the boil; simmer for one minute while stirring. Remove from the heat and cool, blend in an electric blender until smooth, and sieve to get the date bits out. Put the sieved mixture back in the blender with the rest of the milk, the banana, and the wheatgerm, and process until creamy-smooth.

Cashew Nut Topping

2 oz (50 g) unroasted cashew nuts
2 fl oz (50 ml) natural yoghurt
2 teaspoons clear honey

Grind up the cashew nuts as finely as you can, and then blend with the yoghurt and honey until smooth and creamy. Adding a little rose-flower water or a mashed-up banana makes the topping even yummier.

Peanut Shake

peanut butter
vanilla ice-cream
milk

Put equal quantities of all three ingredients into the blender and woosh them together. This is nutritious and delicious.

Chapter Four

Creative Frenzy!

Art, art, art – oh, the agony and the ecstasy of creation ... especially if you are creating a four-storey house with a cake of soap and three drops of poster paint...

At our house we like to think that the gilded paintbrush of fate has touched us, mainly because Peaches' godfather is a painter. Fifi's godfather is a famous dress designer but so far none of has been scuttling down to the kitchen creating haute couture. No doubt one day we'll get the urge. But having a proper PAINTER sending Peaches all manner of pens, pencils and other delights has definitely increased our output artistically.

Arty talk is almost guaranteed to send me apoplectic. Sadly my husband, who is genuinely knowledgeable about art, married the kind of woman one dreads standing near at the Francis Bacon opening, the kind who keeps loudly insisting her three year old could have done all the paintings with a pair of knickers over her head and all the lights off. I adore our artist friend because he doesn't claim that his new collection is all green and mauve because those were the colours that made his heart sing, rather, those colours were the only ones left on the palette at the time and he'd missed the shops. This is refreshing in the world of art.

Not that one's children will talk about any part of themselves singing very much, but they can dip their brushes into paint from a very early age and soon you'll find that you are getting seriously short of wall space as you show off these explosions of creativity.

Art and crafts at home are excellent antidotes to the dreaded What'll-we-do-next syndrome, and who knows, you could be breeding a new generation of naïve artists...

Last week Peaches' godfather came to see her and told us he was about to be hung in every major gallery on the planet – which worried the girls. He also mentioned that he was now the subject of a BBC 2 documentary, so I asked him what he liked about being on TV. He replied that mainly he liked the way they kept giving him his train fares in cash at the end of each day, which I suspect was not quite the answer Melvyn Bragg would have been after.

As your child sets about printing with lino, potatoes, tomatoes and herself, and squirting soap-flakes at paper stuck on to the garden fence, it's worth remembering that Frank Lloyd Wright said he realised he wanted to be an architect before he even went to school when his mother gave him a set of building blocks complete with pediments and columns. Your child may just be the next Jackson Pollock ...

GETTING DOWN TO BASICS

At first you'll have to be satisfied with a kind of unstructured level of art work – one and two year olds are not yet very co-ordinated and are therefore limited in what they can create – paper cutting and very neat brush strokes are out for the moment. They enjoy experimenting – give them glue and a few lentils and they'll make something interesting – probably on their forehead. Give them glitter and glue and the results will be even more spectacular. Those exuberant scribbling sessions with felt-tips will be followed by the life and death struggle to persuade your child to put the lid back on after use. (My advice is to give up now, and put it back yourself.) Two year olds can start their sculpting careers with Play-Doh fruit baskets or animals.

Your art box This needn't be packed with particularly expensive things (although some are essential and do cost money). A lot of the things you'll need for a really good big art box are everyday objects. Here are some suggestions:

chicken wire or florist's wire; wood shavings; paper clips; paper fasteners; paper; dry pasta shapes; bits of sponge or foam; cotton wool; corks; cotton reels; beads; buttons; boxes of any shape or dimension; plastic containers; cardboard tubes from toilet rolls; egg boxes; glitter; children's paintbrushes; children's non-toxic glue; milk bottle tops; straws, Sellotape (both single- and double-sided); school-sized containers of poster paints; powder paints; ceramic paints; coloured tissue paper; big fat crayons; chalks (you can buy blackboard paint for a wall from hardware shops); pencils; non-toxic wash-out felt-tips; empty roll-on deodorant containers; fur fabric; confetti; shells; seeds; sticks; postcards; old greeting cards; old glossy magazines and catalogues.

MODELLING

Play-Doh The smell of this is wonderfully evocative – a mere whiff is enough to send most parents into a trance remembering childhood sessions making baskets of flowers and bananas. Play-Doh now comes with a variety of new-fangled accessories for the modern child. Our children have a Play-Doh mop-top hair salon – you stuff hollow heads with Play-Doh, press the plunger, and out shoot wild Afro hairstyles in acid-trip colours. We've come a long way from making a pear and thinking that was pretty avant-garde!

Home-made Play-Doh I Flour and water; a little salt and a little oil are all that you need. Mix from two parts of flour to every one of salt and water, plus a tablespoon of oil. There are two ways of adding colour to the mixture, either knead a few drops of the food colouring straight into the Play-Doh, which will make it streaky, or add the colouring to the water before you knead it all together for a smooth and even colour. If your Play-Doh dries up, just add a little oil and water and knead thoroughly.

Stretchy Play-Doh II This won't last very long – but if you want Play-Doh with stretch appeal use self-raising flour instead of plain.

Scented Play-Doh You might like to try adding a few drops of flavouring – peppermint, for example – to make it smell! Scented Play-Doh's more suitable for an older pre-schooler, as a toddler will just want to eat it, and you'll spend the whole session trying to stop her from cramming it into her mouth...

Very long-lasting Play-Doh III Use the recipe for Home-made Play-Doh I, but add to it two teaspoons of cream of tartar. Mix it up to a smooth paste and then put it into a pan and cook it slowly until it comes away from the sides. When it is cool, take it out and knead

it well. At this stage it's ready for use and will last a long time in an air-tight container. Wash up your pan as this Play-Doh will stick and go weird!

Clay Real clay is a different consistency to Play-Doh, heavier and less malleable. When buying real clay make sure that it is non-toxic. To stop it from going hard, you'll have to keep it in a metal or a plastic container with a proper lid, together with a metal nailfile for slicing bits off at playing time.

Make snakes, snails, worms, snowmen, fruits, vegetables, pancakes, trays with cups on, bears, cats, dogs, frogs – even caterpillars! A session with biscuit cutters can turn a piece of clay into parts of a mobile for attaching to a coat-hanger. With a pencil, press a hole for the thread into the top of each part before it dries.

A more professional clay If you're feeling ambitious why not try the kind of modelling clay now available that sets totally rock solid when the model's left out overnight. You don't have to fire the model, and it can be varnished and painted with rather spectacular and professional results. Your child will be able to make splendid plates, ashtrays, small bowls and vases.

Salt dough To make this, you need two cups of flour; one cup of salt; and one cup of water. This will also go hard if left out overnight, but putting the models in a low oven for several hours will harden them best. With the help of some florist's wire you can make great Christmas decorations with this dough. Use the wire to make little hooks for the ornaments then paint or glitter them. Children will enjoy making Christmas trees, stars or small balls. Or try threading salt-dough beads on to a string or a piece of elastic. Make sure you knot the end thoroughly to start your child off, or threading will be a frustrating experience! Or make a paperweight in a simple shape and in a largish size. Stars or fish go down well and squiggles and scales can be gouged out of the dough to great effect.

Soap sculptures If you haven't made Play-Doh and don't want to buy modelling clay, look in the cupboard – you've probably got soap-flakes.

87

Mix half a cup of hot water to two cups of soap-flakes and a little powder paint or food colouring, then beat it all up with an electric mixer.

Your child will need to dip her hands into warm water before she starts to model the soap into shapes, and it is easier to move them if you put them on to a sheet of foil. Soap sculptures will last for weeks, they are particularly effective at Christmas, as they make good snowmen, and if the soap mix is stuck on to a pine cone it looks like snow . . .

Papier Mâché This is a long process best tackled over several afternoons, and with an older child. Children can get frustrated waiting for the results; you might prefer to make the papier mâché base yourself and let your child decorate it, thereby preventing total loss of interest in the project or furious whining!

Papier mâché means mashed paper. The first thing that you have to do is tear lots of sheets of newspaper into smallish rectangles, then spread Vaseline over the smallish bowl that you'll be using as a mould. This stops the bowl being permanently trapped in your papier mâché! Cover the plate or bowl with overlapping bits of newspaper so that the entire surface is totally hidden, then cover it with wallpaper paste and another layer of newspaper. Leave that for five or six hours to set hard. You have to do this until there are six to eight layers of newspaper all over the plate. Then take the papier mâché plate off the real one using a knife, and trim around the edge of the plate to make it smooth. Finally, paste more paper over the bottom of the plate where the Vaseline was.

Another idea is to use rainbow-coloured tissue paper pasted on in the same way as the newspaper, in layers, in order to achieve depth of colour and texture.

When it comes to decoration, a really spectacular effect can be achieved if you give your child a small pot of gold paint and some old wrapping paper. Paint the papier mâché bowl gold all over, then once that has dried stick pictures cut from the wrapping paper on to the surface. We used roses and peonies. Varnish the bowl to a high gloss. Don't worry if your child is not particularly good at using scissors yet. Just let her rip small pictures or patterns out of paper – the effect is just as good.

Other papier mâché ideas To make a papier mâché balloon, blow up a large balloon, and then cover it in newspaper strips and wallpaper paste. You'll need to allow one or two days for it to dry completely, depending on how many layers of newspaper you were patient enough to use! Then paint and varnish it. Why not go one step further with your creation and make it into a floating fish or bird by adding streamers for a tail or wings. You could then hang the creatures from your child's bedroom ceiling.

Try converting your papier mâché balloon into a *piñata* for a party. Make a small hole in it, burst the original balloon and pull it out through the gap. Fill the papier mâché ball with sweets. Hang it from the ceiling. Have fun at the party by blindfolding the guests and getting them to take turns hitting the *piñata* with a stick until all the sweets pour out on to the ground!

A set of papier mâché skittles is easy to make. You'll need six or eight empty plastic cordial bottles, some sand and a funnel. First make the skittles' heads with a rolled-up ball of newspaper, making sure you give each one a neck that will fit into the top of the cordial bottle. Next, half-fill each bottle with sand by pouring the sand through the funnel. Cover the bottle (and its head) with papier mâché in the usual way. Wait until the layers of paper are completely dry before you paint the skittles. You can personalise the skittles by painting on faces of familiar people, and making hair for them out of raffia or straw. Then you can take turns rolling a ball at the skittles and adding up the scores!

To make a papier mâché bangle, all you need to do is cover segments of a cardboard loo-roll tube with the layers of paste and paper. If the loo-roll tube doesn't fit your child's wrist, use a strip of card with the ends stapled together. Again, paint and varnish, and if you like stick on glitter, false jewels or sequins. Even tinsel looks effective.

PRINTING

Potato prints These are very simple although the first time I did them with Fifi she ate the potato before we'd even got started. Cut the potato in half, then cut it so that your design is the raised part of the potato. Stars, triangles, cubes, circles, and letters are all easy. The other half should be something that fits correspondingly with your design – the tail of a shooting star, the bucket for a triangular Christmas tree. Give your child the two halves, two small dishes of poster paint to dip them into and a large sheet of paper. Now she's ready to press her prints all over the place.

Leaf prints Paint one side of the leaf with poster paint, then place the leaf paint-side down on a sheet of paper and press with the flat of your hand. For a clearer print place another sheet of paper over the painted leaf and press that firmly – the print will be on the first sheet and will smudge less that way.

Vegetable printing Cut a fruit or a vegetable and drain away the juice. Tomatoes and oranges are excellent printers.

Sponge printing Use lots of small thick sponges cut into simple shapes for pressing on to the sheet.

Clay prints Use salt dough and make a set of shapes.
    These need to be reasonably thick so that a child can hold them to make the print. Press them into the paint and print!

Stencil printing for beginners As there is always a certain amount of mess when any child is splattering paint around, it's best to do this outside! Go out on a walk and collect leaves, flowers, and grass, or other things with interesting shapes. Lay them out on a large sheet of paper, cover this with a sheet of wire meshing, and then dip an old toothbrush into poster paint and drag it back and forth across the wire meshing. Allow the paint to dry and remove the leaves. You'll be left with the outlines.

Tennis ball printing Just stick a large sheet of paper against the garden fence, dip tennis balls into paint and throw them. Very small children will enjoy rolling paint-covered balloons over the paper instead.

DYEING FOR FUN AT HOME!

Dyeing fabric means fast, spectacular, vivid results which of course give everyone a feeling of accomplishment. Fabric dyes can be bought at the chemist's and are inexpensive and relatively easy to use. It's wise to do it outside if weather permits (then again I always say that because I'm *always* the one left with the globs of dye dripping down the paintwork).

A multicoloured effect For dyeing extravaganzas at home I use cold-water dyes, which I buy in several of the very brightest shades. I find that green, pink, purple and red work best together, although you may need sunglasses to look at it all afterwards. We tested our efforts out on my husband's underpants, the results of which went down like a lead balloon . . .

Fold up a T-shirt or just a plain sheet of white cotton until it is a tiny square, then dip each of the four corners into a different bowl of cold dye. Wait until it's all dried, and unfold. (Do not forget to squeeze out excess dye after each application, and let the colours meet in the central panel of your fabric.)

The ultimate sixties effect You'll need cold-water dyes in about three colours; dye fixative; white cotton T-shirt or a piece of fabric; rubber gloves for both of you and string. After you've prepared the dyes in separate containers, bunch up the fabric or garment and then tie very very very tight string around it at intervals. Put on rubber gloves and immerse the material or garment into one of the solutions. Remove and allow to semi-dry. Now you can take off the string and admire the effect. Allow to dry completely before you repeat the process with new string and a different colour, then you can do it all again with another colour if you wish.

Design a T-shirt With a fabric-dye pen, draw a design on a T-shirt. It will work best on a plain white one.

ARTISTIC INSPIRATIONS

Collage This means sticking lots of different things on to a large board or paper, anything from pictures from a catalogue to ribbons and sequins. Children just in from a walk can make a collage of leaves they've collected. Anything works as long as it isn't too heavy for the paper.

Make sure you have a table to sit at, with your child at a comfortable height. It's no use trying to create great art if you're peering up at the paper getting neck-ache.

For big things – like making a long mural together, maybe of the seaside or the park with sky and clouds and real leaves on the trees and scrunched up blue tissue paper dipped into glue for the ponds – you'll need to get down on the floor and obviously the kitchen is the least likely place to end up ruined by any spills.

Once little children are past the age when they put everything into their mouths they will enjoy collage very much, adding stickers willy-nilly and gluing on bits and pieces with abandon. Small children are better not trying to do anything realistic, but will love making patterns.

Children who have trouble manipulating brushes and fine felt-tips may enjoy trying something a little more free form. Get a big sheet of lining paper and spread trickles of children's glue all over it.

Give your child glitter, salt, rice, and confetti for her to stick on. When she's finished, put all the excess into a container ready for another time. Let the picture dry thoroughly before you hang it up.

The tactile element of collage is important to a child; why not try using dried fruits, nuts, lentils or beans. Cut out painted paper and rolled-up newspaper to create a scene. The bigger the better. Or go completely abstract and create a collage from different types of string.

Finger-painting I read in one excellent book that children who do finger-painting to soothing music get very relaxed, it's such a therapeutic activity! Certainly, dipping your hands – if not all of you – into soft squishy paint is an interesting sensory experience. It has to be said that some children think finger-painting too messy, and don't like to get their hands dirty! They can, however, be eased into it if you experiment with different textures of paint...

It's wise before you start to have some rules to prevent the mess overpowering the fun of it, especially if you are hoping it's going to be relaxing for both of you. Strip your child if it's warm, alternatively, put her in a protective wrap of apron with sleeves, tell her not to wander around when she is painting, and have a washing-up bowl of soapy water at the ready for cleaning her up when she gets bored.

The paper that you use needs to be heavy enough to rub with your paint-drenched hands without it becoming a sodden mess and ripping.

A good paint for finger-painting can be made from one part starch granules; two parts boiling water; and a few drops of food colouring. Add a little water to the starch to make a paste, then add the hot water to the starch, continuously stirring it until it's thick, and then adding the colour. Give it to your children to mess with while it's a little warm for another effect.

Duplicate your efforts by printing your finger-painting on to another sheet of paper. Do your wild and swirling best, then press a clean sheet of paper on top of your painting. You'll be left with a clear print.

Invisible pictures Draw a picture on paper with an ordinary white candle. As you paint the paper (using a paintbrush) your wax picture will magically emerge. You can use black crayon instead of the candle, but it's not quite so mysterious.

Don't be restricted to a paintbrush Small foam rollers, sponges, and bits of string dipped thickly in paint make good alternatives.

Spray-painting If you have some of those sprays for watering begonias with a thin mist, you could try filling them up with paints,

covering your garden fence in lining paper and letting the kids spray-paint it. If it's wet and you've got a few children around, spray-painting on a front window can look wonderful. Powder paint has the most vivid colours and is also easy to wash off.

A body painting Get hold of a very large sheet of paper and try a portrait of your child by your child ... All you have to do is draw around your child as she lies on the paper, then she can draw in all her own personal details, and paint them, too. Cut out the picture and play with it.

Blow splatters Paint liquid starch on to paper, then paint directly on to the paper with *dry* powder paint – or blow it through a straw.

Crayon magic Of course you don't have to use paints to create interesting effects. Crayon lots and lots of layers of different colours on a sheet of paper, topping it off with a thick layer of black crayon. Now 'draw' your picture on it with the end of a paintbrush or a hair-grip, scraping at the paper to create a multicoloured line.

A joint mural If it's a wet afternoon, there are a few children around and you've a lot of paper (a long, long sheet) you could get them to work on a mural based on a theme. For example, they could each choose a different time of the day and draw or paint what they are usually doing at this time.

A new kind of paint Here's a use for the old washing-up liquid bottles you've been keeping! Mix equal parts of flour and salt and then add poster paint to it to form a paste. Pour this mixture into the bottles. Squeeze the paint-mix out into a pattern or a picture, but make sure the paper's strong enough to take it!

Soap paint Mix up half a cup of cold water with one cup of soap-flakes. Add some poster paint, then mix with an electric mixer to a fairly stiff consistency. Paint on to white paper.

BEAUTIFUL MOBILES

A sea monster of the deep! By now you'll be aware of the need to preserve such valuable items as the clear plastic container your chicken noodle soup came in last Friday night ... This kind of container makes a great basis for a monster of the deep – which can be strung up in front of your toddler's bedroom window so that the light shines through it.

The 'monster' is really more of a jelly fish. We made ours in pale-pink tissue paper. Cut the lid of the plastic container in half and glue the two halves together to form a half-moon shape, then cover that with glue. Cover this completely with crushed pink tissue paper. There should be about six inches of paper left hanging loose from the flat side of the shape. Cut this into tendrils to form the monster's tentacles. Glue on eyes cut out of white paper.

A tropical fish This looks wonderful and if you make it successfully it can also be used as a kite on blustery days. You'll need a foil bag (the kind used as liners for wines and juices); a large, very brightly coloured plastic shopping bag; two plastic cups; string; stapler; scissors; and paper fasteners.

Cut both ends off the plastic foil liner and chop off the tap bit too, which is the end that will form the tail. Then carefully cut the rim off a plastic plate and staple the rim around the top of the liner to form the mouth of your fish!

Staple some tucks into the bottom end of the liner and cut your large plastic bag into a fringe. Make sure that the other end is not shredded so that it can be neatly attached to the bottom of the bag to make a wildly tropical tail. Attach some fringe to the side of your fish to give it fins. The bottoms of your plastic cups form the eyes (you'll need to felt-tip some big black pupils on). Your child may feel like being really elaborate and adding long eyelashes cut from the plastic bag. Don't forget to make a hole for the string so that you can hang the fish up.

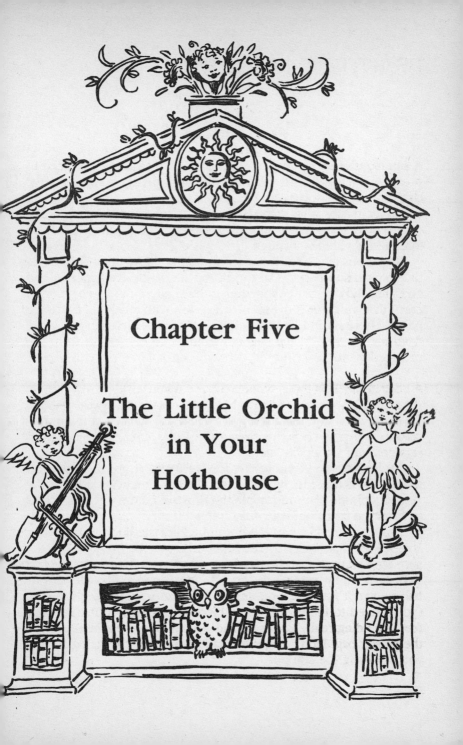

Chapter Five

The Little Orchid in Your Hothouse

Some of us feel that there are many good reasons for delaying the moment when our children start school, although there are children (especially ones on their own at home) who yearn for the camaraderie of kindergarten, and it does give mothers a couple of free hours in the morning. But as long as you're prepared to do lots to encourage them to learn at home, there doesn't seem much point in sending them off to work years earlier than necessary. Lots of nursery schools will take children as soon as they are out of nappies, which strikes me as being much too early.

I'm sure somewhere on the planet there is someone whose eyes fill with fond tears as they recall their old *alma mater*, but I haven't come across any of them. One of my relations was expelled from his school for hitting a priest over the head with a sink – he did it to save his brother from a serious beating at the hands of the crazed Catholic. My husband seems to have spent a large portion of his youth clad in hipsters skiving off school and never regretting it. On the other hand I loathed every second of school but did well which meant that I was allowed to skive off with everyone's blessing!

Not that I haven't attempted to instil into my own daughters at least a modicum of interest in school: they'll have to go, so why not make the most of the experience. What I have managed to avoid is sending them to any of the many schools I sampled before the age of twelve, while my mother was leading a rather gypsy existence.

At one point I attended the perfect English boarding school, one of those establishments that believed in the spartan life (albeit a spartan life costing one's parents many many thousands of pounds). Pupils lived like inmates at Colditz, regularly forsaking the debating society for escape committees. At this school a lampshade over the ceiling light was one of the many things strictly forbidden. My mother, whose idea of roughing it is a half-pint bottle of Chanel

No 5 rather than a full gallon, could hardly bear the thought of me living under the swinging pendulum of the bare 400-watt bulb. So she sent me a red satin shade with fluffy bobbles hanging off it, of the kind more usually found in Parisian brothels *circa* 1932. It was confiscated. I was rusticated. My mother was corsetted, but then again she always was . . .

The girls were made to wear two pairs of knickers at all times. One pair was white, made out of what appeared to be the lagging most people put around their boiler (aptly enough I suppose), and the others were large, grey-flannel drawers, which had a pocket in them, to keep a ten-pence piece in case a girl was very lost and had to phone the school. Knicker-checks were performed in the corridors if any member of the powers that be suspected you were frolicking along wearing floral M&S pants instead, and they could definitely spot that lightness of step caused by the removal of both heavy layers of drawers.

It's probably no wonder my children are bohemians who skip around naked half the time, after my bottom endured the English public school equivalent of foot-binding for so many years . . .

SPOTTING YOUR CHILD'S POTENTIAL

Intelligence shows itself in different ways, and each child will demonstrate different strengths and abilities. Intelligence can be divided into six broad categories. On identifying your child's particular intelligence (or intelligences), there's a lot you can do to encourage her to make the most of it.

Linguistic intelligence Children who have this find it easy to remember words, and from an early age are memorising nursery rhymes and baby's songs. Such children tend to be early talkers, and once they are talking will be quick to learn how to read and write. This gives them a feeling of great confidence which spills over into other things they attempt to learn. A child with linguistic intelligence will develop a love of books and will enjoy playing word games with you. Have fun with this splendid talent.

Spatial intelligence Signs of this are being able to tackle a shape sorter with no problems, enjoying puzzles and drawing realistically earlier than average. A child will have a good sense of proportion and direction, and be able to visualise patterns and maps. She'll be good at games involving judging distances. Jobs such as engineering, architecture and graphics all require good spatial intelligence.

Musical intelligence A musical child will pick up tunes quickly and have a good sense of rhythm as she bangs the tunes out on toy instruments. She'll have a good ear and be able to sing in tune. She will take to learning an instrument, and her co-ordination and concentration are likely to be good.

Personal intelligence A child with this kind of intelligence will be sensitive to other people's feelings, and be able to relate well to other people's situations from an early age. In later life she will not only make friends easily but will also be a good leader. It's important to talk to her about people and their feelings, and she'll enjoy role-playing games.

Logical-mathematical intelligence Does your child enjoy sorting things according to size, shape and colour? Does she like counting games? Does she ask questions about numbers and their relationship to each other? This kind of child enjoys computers, calculators, and number-related games.

Bodily-kinaesthetic intelligence This shows itself in physical talent: a good sense of balance, learning to pedal a tricycle earlier than is usual, good dancing, skipping, swimming and acrobatics – indeed, any activity requiring co-ordination without tripping! A child with these abilities tends also to be adept at acting and imitating other people; she is observant, alert, and has a good imagination.

THE ATTENTION SPAN OF A GNAT – LEARNING GOOD CONCENTRATION

Poor concentration makes learning very difficult for most children. There are some obvious reasons for poor concentration like feeling tired, ill, starving hungry or just plain bored. However, there are some children who find it difficult to concentrate on any task that is set before them. They'll get up and wander about when you're trying to explain something to them, and sometimes won't even sit still to watch television, astonishing as it may sound. Some parents do have unrealistic expectations of their children and fail to realise that a child of under five can concentrate for little more than five minutes. She won't, for example, be able to paint for much longer than this at a time, although she may be able to listen to a story for ten minutes. By the time your child is at school she'll be able to paint for ten minutes, model clay for fifteen minutes, and by the time she is seven take in and discuss information for twenty to twenty-five minutes.

Everyone remembers being told to pay attention by the teacher. Paying attention is the first part of learning, and if your child isn't encouraged to learn how to do it, she's going to find learning much harder once she gets to school.

Keep the demon TV at bay Actually, that's pretty rich coming from me, an adult with almost completely square eyeballs, whose one ambition since I've had a few children is to spend several days in bed, not ill at all, eating Thornton's Continental Selection and watching TV, preferably continuous *Inspector Morse*. However, my ambition is yet to be achieved (and won't be in the next decade or so) which means I'm allowed to be bitter and twisted about the innocent box when it comes to children.

Television does little or nothing to help a child's concentration, and it can become a complete substitute for reading and conversation. If my eldest daughter is anything to go by, a completely stupid cartoon of the absolutely most *tacky* kind can take priority over almost anything as she cranes closer and closer to the screen, completely mesmerised. She would happily sit with all her pals in complete darkness on a roasting hot summer's day watching rugby union if I let her, but I'm cruel and strict about this one. We've got a rule in our house that TV can only be watched if the children can actually name a specific programme. The exception is on Saturday mornings when they can watch what they like and also indulge themselves in sweets. Saturday mornings must be nirvana to them – sugar and *Scooby-Do* all in one go!

Concentration games Help your child develop good concentration by playing games with her that involve remembering pictures: Lotto and snap, for example. There are many activity books available containing pictures to colour, lines to join up, simple puzzles to do, all of which will give your child good concentration practice. Don't leave a child who has concentration problems on her own with a game or picture, but stay with her while she does them. At first, just spend a short time together at these tasks, and don't forget to praise her as she goes along. During these shared activities, you may have to repeat your instructions, as remembering them may be the hardest thing your child has to master. Look at her while you're showing her what to do – and stay patient!

HELP YOUR CHILD TO UNDERSTAND TIME

From the minute our children arrive we start teaching them the difference between day and night. Gradually, a routine evolves, and eventually children acquire a concept of days, weeks, months and years. A long time before they can tell the time, children will ask questions about it along the lines of, How long till we get to the park? How long till Christmas? and so on. When you explain how many minutes it will take they completely flummox you by asking, after a pensive silence, how long a minute is.

Although children of around three like to talk about annual events like their birthday, by the time they are four they have a sense of what time in the day certain things happen. They know what time they go to bed and what time they go to playschool, for example. They still won't be able to tell the time on a clock, so now's a good moment to start teaching them.

Teaching your child to tell the time The first thing to do is invest in a children's book about time. The Ladybird *My Day* and *Telling the Time* are excellent. Another useful prop is a model clock, which you can make yourself out of a paper plate. Attach a long and a short hand made out of cardboard to the clock face with a paper fastener. Start by showing your child how time on the hour is shown: one o'clock etc. Then move on to the half hour and the quarters, and so on.

What is a minute? The next time that you are making your child a boiled egg, put her in charge of the egg timer, and explain that it takes three minutes for the sand to pour through the little funnel. Or set the alarm on your bedside clock to go off after a minute. However, if you both just sit on the bed waiting for the alarm to go off, a minute will seem like a lifetime. It is better to set her an interesting task and ask her to see if she can complete it before the alarm goes off.

The easiest way to explain seconds (and that a minute is made up of seconds) is to time your child as she runs round the garden or the park. Loudly count out the seconds as she goes. Next, get her to do the same distance walking and compare the number of seconds it takes.

Months and seasons Although pre-school children don't have much concept of months, most of them do take a keen interest in the weather, probably because it's the weather that determines how they're going to spend their day. Children soon realise that different seasons have different weather: cold at Christmas and hot in the summer. Use this understanding of seasons to start teaching your child the months. As well as reciting them to her and getting her to repeat them, why not make a season chart. Invest in a large roll of wallpaper-lining paper and tape together two large sheets of this. Mark on to it four separate areas. Settle down on the sofa in front of the fire with a teetering pile of magazines, seed brochures and old Christmas cards and choose a selection of pictures for each season. Glue these pictures on to the paper and make a frenziedly coloured collage for your wall. Spring could be a riot of Easter eggs, bunnies and daffodils; summer, sunshine and beaches; autumn, a harvest selection of fruits and vegetables, and autumn leaves; winter, pictures from old Christmas cards.

A weekly diary Most two year olds can be taught to recite the days of the week, but soon they start to realise that different days mean different events. Quite small children understand that some days Daddy will be at home all day, and some days not, for example. Making a diary together gives them more understanding still. You'll need seven very large pieces of paper. Staple these into book form and divide each page into two sections. At the end of each day, fill in the diary with your child, writing the day of the week at the top. Underneath your child could draw a picture of what she's enjoyed most during the day. The two of you could write a short sentence about the day's activities to go with the picture. At the end of the

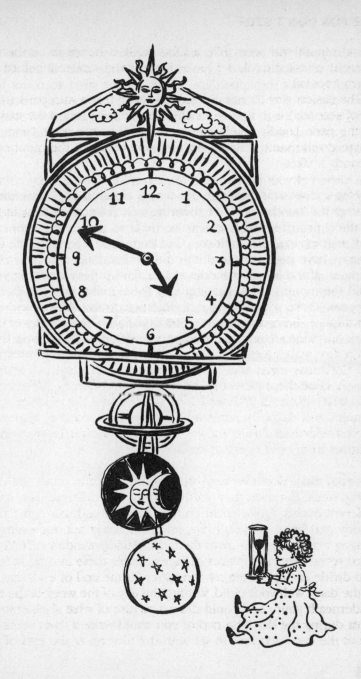

month, you'll be able to compare weeks and days – what was unusual or exciting and what remained the same. If something special is about to happen you could use the diary to count how many days your child has to wait. However, if there's a particularly long wait involved, you can help convey the passage of time by saying, for example, first there's your birthday, then it's the summer holiday, and then the new baby arrives.

A wallchart of your daily routine Most families have a daily routine that varies very little, with the day being punctuated by mealtimes. One of the easiest ways of conveying to a child an understanding of the times these daily events occur is to make an ornamental wallchart of your daily activities and their time. You'll need a very long, narrow piece of paper. On the left-hand side ask your child to draw all the things she does that make up the routine, starting with getting up in the morning and ending with going to bed in the evening. Your job is to draw a clock beside each picture showing the time of each event: seven o'clock, wake up; eight o'clock, have breakfast; nine o'clock, get dressed; ten o'clock, go to the park etc.

THE JOYS OF BOOKS

Reading to your child is one of the great pleasures of being a parent. Introducing her to the world of reading, even if she is still a baby, is to introduce her to a joy that lasts and lasts. It's a marvellous opportunity to be intimate whilst at the same time teaching your child a great deal. Books mirror familiar experiences and introduce your child to fresh ones. They extend her vocabulary and fire her imagination. Reading together isn't just something for those odd off-days that every mother knows.

Books are everyday objects It's a good plan, once your child is mobile, to put her books within easy reach so that she can bring one to you when she feels like it or just sit on the floor and look at them herself, learning to turn a page at a time and enjoying the pictures. Inevitably, some books will get mangled. It takes time for a toddler to understand that books have to be treated gently, and in eagerness and excitement the odd cover has been known to get torn off, but that's all part of the process of getting used to books and understanding that they're an everyday part of life.

Her changing tastes When you read to a one year old, it doesn't matter if the story is a bit advanced for her age, you can just paraphrase it in your own words. Or try Janet and Allan Ahlberg's *The Baby's Catalogue* and *Peepo!* The Richard Scarry books go down well at this age because they have so many small pictures.

By the age of two you will probably have discovered that you are living with a whirlwind, a miniature Mussolini who wants her own way and wants it fast! During this frenetic time, books become even more important to your child. They'll also be important to you in providing an opportunity for a few moments of quiet time with your child before she embarks on her investigation of the drainage system. Two year olds who have trouble settling down at night will love a bedtime story, snuggled in their beds with a peachy glow enfolding you both and a rip-roaring yarn enfolding. By now your child will enjoy a proper story – try Shirley Hughes's 'Alfie' books, or her delightful 'Lucy and Tom' stories.

By the time you have what may appear to be a rather civilised three year old you'll be able to read her books with plots. There'll be endless interruptions for questions about why people in the story are doing and saying what they are and about the meaning of words. Despite the fact your child is likely to be using fairly simple words and sentences, she'll be capable of understanding more of a story, and appreciate the fantasy world of old-fashioned fairy stories and adventure stories such as *Little Tim and the Brave Sea Captain* by Edward Ardizzone.

By four your child will be perfecting her many new skills and abilities; she'll be more aware and more independent. This goes hand in hand with being more imaginative, and able to put herself in other people's shoes. If your child is *very* imaginative, though, she will be easily frightened. It's not a good idea to read really spooky or scary stories to her. Tales about wolves eating little pigs raw can make such a child go rigid with fear, and no amount of reassurance along the lines of there being few wolves in downtown Cricklewood will do any good, once she's been made to feel insecure by hearing a vivid tale.

A four- and five-year-old child will love joining the library and visiting the children's section, and will, no doubt, insist on making her own selection. But not before she has removed every single book from the shelves and received several choice scowls from the librarian. I can only say that children who go to cafés and restaurants from an early age tend to behave marginally less like animals at feeding time at the zoo, and the same applies to getting used to the local library.

By now, books will be an integral part of your child's life, and she will have her firm favourites. The Stan and Jan Berenstain 'Bear' books are a delight, and Fifi still sometimes picks one up. The stories are about a family of bears, Mum, Dad, and daughter, and their domestic dramas: nail-biting; bad dreams, a bad school report, bullying, a disappointing holiday. There are about thirty titles in the paperback series, and each one is hugely enjoyable. That's when you know a book choice has been a real success – when over and over again your child picks up that book and hands it lovingly to you with the inevitable cry, *Read it again!*

LEARNING TO READ AND WRITE AT HOME

The Glen Doman reading method I strongly recommend this (if you think that you have the time and aptitude for teaching your child to read). *Teach Your Baby to Read* by Glen Doman is a complete kit with everything you'll need to get your budding intellectual at it by the age of three! As soon as your child is able to talk you can start. By using loads of flash cards of words, you will teach your child to recognise them and tell you what they are. It's up to you to make this daily ritual *fun*! Peaches is learning to read this way at the moment, and loves it. Anyone would think 'toe' was the most thrilling word in the universe as I wave the red-and-white flash card at Peaches at least six times a day. I imagine she also learns that her family is barking mad!

A variation on this method is to use picture postcards. Get your child to match the picture to another card with the word written on it.

At the end of the course she will be able to read the simple book that comes with the kit, which of course will give any small child an enormous feeling of confidence and achievement. It really is onwards and upwards after that.

The phonetic approach to reading This a popular method, but, as a devotee of the 'look-and-say' method, I think it's probably harder. What it entails is learning to recognise letters and their sounds, then building up words from the different sounds. Unfortunately, there are so many exceptions to the rule in the English language that it's often quite hard to beat your way to the final answer! However, if you want to use this method, games are a great aid to learning. Try a simple game of I-spy, where instead of using the letter-name you give its sound instead.

Learning the alphabet Why not make your own alphabet book, illustrating the letters with pictures of your child's favourite things.

It's hard to beat the old-fashioned way of learning the alphabet. Just repeat it over and over again and your child will in time remember it.

Learning to write Once your child has made some headway in recognising words (and/or sounds) and the alphabet is becoming less of a mystery, you can start to make a game out of learning to write – which isn't easy, as there are twenty-six letters to learn, as well as the capitals. At first, concentrate on developing her manual dexterity so that she can successfully manipulate a pencil. After that – more of the old-fashioned approach! Make sure that the two of you have a quiet, peaceful spot to work in, and that there's a lot of patience (and reward!) coming from you. Coax her into copying the letters over and over again. Or encourage her to write over dot-to-dot letters, or to trace letters.

Children love being able to write their name, and you can make learning this into an artistic pursuit, writing each letter on a big piece of paper and then filling in the outline with glue so that your child can decorate it however she wants. Pin the name up in her bedroom.

DRIVE YOURSELF MAD WITH MATHS

I really wish now I'd taught Fifi her tables before she went to school, instead of struggling to drill them into her now when there are so many other exciting things to distract her.

To be quite honest, my grasp of the world of numbers is so shaky as to be almost non-existent, but I have managed to teach several small children to count up to twenty . . . You may manage far greater feats with your pre-schooler, but I'm afraid I still don't know my eight-times table and can become almost apoplectic trying to work out fractions. Repetition is the secret to teaching a basic feel for numbers and a sense of sequence, and the best way to do it is through songs with numbers in them like 'On the First Day of Christmas', 'Ten Green Bottles', 'One Man Went to Mow', 'There Were Ten in the Bed', for example. Endless singing of these songs – on the bus, on the way to the park, in the bath – will do the trick. A game of number-I-spy is a good idea, as is teaching your child to use weighing scales, to dial a number on the phone; and playing dice and card games. Try playing Shop; this is the perfect opportunity for number-learning. Mark groceries with prices and practise adding and taking-away sums as you calculate the bill and the change.

Don't miss an opportunity Count the stairs whenever you both go up and down – indeed, count everything! At teatime say, One for you, one for me; count your child's toys out when you are playing together; count whenever you can. Having said that, numbers still give me a migraine, and Fifi's homework makes me feel like something out of *The Manchurian Candidate*!

NIJINSKY ON YOUR DOORSTEP

Every parent likes to mention to their child that Mozart composed wonders when he was seven, and most of us will have noticed how musical small children are until they reach the stage of becoming horribly self-conscious and watching one too many programmes of *Top of the Pops*.

English people tend not to be great dancers, unless they dance professionally. Skip into the nearest nightclub, or peer through the curtains at a party one night, and you'll see many many young men in light-blue Crimplene shirts, having what looks like a serious attack of nerves as they lunge wildly across the room pointing their fingers at the ceiling and frugging furiously. The eroticism of dance has not hit many Rotary Club dinner dances; even Prince Charles, one of Britain's greatest objects of eroticism, always does that utterly British dance with his bottom sticking out slightly.

I am to the dance-floor what Bernard Manning is to the body stocking. I rarely, if ever, dance, and if I do it's usually under cover of darkness and alone. I'm so busy concentrating every fibre of my being on keeping (somehow) in time with the record that's playing that I couldn't possibly hope to be in time with another person as well, not without months of practice. I also have the most appalling luck with the people who ask me to dance. For some reason men imagine that I'm the woman who taught John Travolta all his more astonishing moves, so I'm always asked to dance by the only person in the club who can do the splits on a four-foot-square dance floor. I'd be much happier dancing round my handbag with four other girls, miming words to the 'Birdie Song', than attempting a triple-back somersault with a bronzed Adonis who teaches the rumba part time. My children have none of these problems – if they watch a Kylie Minogue video once they can do all the dances immediately (and in perfect time) and if someone starts drilling the road outside with any rhythm then they'll dance to that too.

117

Dance classes Lots of pre-schoolers get enrolled for ballet classes. Ballet dancing as a career has a low rate of success, so it should be emphasised that for under-fives ballet should be just for the fun of dancing, music, and meeting other toddlers. It spoils it if there is pressure to pass grades and exams – at this age just tying the ribbons on your ballet slippers can be challenge enough.

There are also lots of classes available in music and movement, tap and jazz, in fact almost any sort of dancing you can think of from Irish, Scottish and Turkish to the ever more exotic. A lot of local councils run day classes for mothers and children so the two of you can learn to dance together.

You don't have to spend a lot of money if you decide to take up dancing, but it's wise to remember that lots of dance studios tend to be chilly. Buy your child a dance bolero to wear over her vest and knickers, as it has to be said that a leotard does look a little odd over a quilted liberty bodice ... Ballet shoes wear out quickly but to begin with you'll probably find that your child doesn't need to wear any shoes at all.

If you don't like the idea of organised dance classes, just turn on a tape at home and the two of you can dance together to your hearts' content. Toddlers love copying dances, and are terrific hams in front of the mirror. Dancing at home is a good way of releasing tensions – if you're both having a bad day, dance it off. Express all the emotions you've been bottling up. Pretend you're your old teacher at school, the one who (at least twice a week) made everyone in the youngest class pretend they were little bushes in a high wind. Encourage your child to dance-act scenes from stories and rhymes.

Try combining dancing with exercising and buy one of those horrendously punishing exercise videos – toddlers adore them. She'll happily join you as you spend time trying to locate muscles you never realised you had before the two of you collapse on to the sofa and reach for the nearest toffee tin. Make sure there are lots of toys and books near by, as sensible toddlers get bored before the end of a tape!

MAKING MUSIC

Listening to music is an integral part of many adults' lives. Naturally, children will absorb the sounds and continue to enjoy music in adult life. You don't need to be able to play an instrument or sing well to help a child discover the pleasures of music. She'll get a lot out of just listening to the music you enjoy, as well as music aimed at children. If you want to be more actively encouraging, there's plenty of scope.

Action songs These are great favourites with toddlers. They'll love marching to 'The Grand Old Duke of York', and singing songs like 'The Wheels of the Bus', which is a song that can be made to seem endless by adapting it to encompass the entire family and their particular foibles! 'Heads, Fingers, Knees and Toes' is another good song as it teaches small children to identify the parts of the body at the same time – and is riotous! Then there are all the nursery rhymes, and Christmas songs, and counting songs. It's well worth buying a book of children's songs because in my experience you start off confidently with the first three lines and then realise, to your humiliation, that you don't know any more.

A toddler music group Play music together with a collection of home-made instruments. They're very easy to make.

Cut a coconut in half and you have two clappers ready to be painted and varnished by your child.

A xylophone can be improvised by filling half a dozen milk bottles with different amounts of water and then hitting the bottles with a stick to make the sounds.

Make a drum out of an empty tin with a piece of thick paper spread across the top and taped into place.

Shakers can be made from tins or boxes filled with buttons, pebbles or pasta shells.

Then there is the old comb and paper ... or make chimes from different metal objects hung up with string. Hit them with a stick and they'll make a note.

Learning an instrument the Suzuki way If you really think that your child shows an aptitude for music and she seems keen to learn, then you might consider the Suzuki method. Children from the age of two and a half can learn the violin, piano or cello this way. They do not learn through written music but by playing games, listening to records, and copying songs. Learning an instrument this way does involve a lot of practising, but it is done in little bouts so that children don't get bored. Suzuki children learn to play a tune very quickly so that from an early stage they have a sense of achievement!

THIS SPORTING LIFE

It's not a good idea to thrust pre-schoolers into competitive sports. Children hate the pressure, and it spoils sports for them for ever, making them feel that winning is the only thing that matters, and not enjoyment.

Miniature sports Throughout the country it is possible to enrol quite small children at sports centres where they can make the most of the facilities on offer. Why not try some of the scaled-down versions of adult sports like basketball, football and tennis. Your child will get some healthy exercise, develop her physical co-ordination, and above all have fun. From a parent's point of view such activities are great for exhausting your child afterwards and ensuring you of a little peace!

Your local town hall will be able to supply details of miniature sports facilities available in your area, as well as gyms and swimming pools.

Tumble Tots Most toddlers will enjoy being budding Olga Korbuts. At Tumble Tots they can have their first experience of gymnastics, donning leotards and doing simple exercises, music and movement, and going through simple obstacle courses. And it's another great way of getting to know other children of the same age.

Tumble Tots, 15 Borough High Street, London SE1 9SE.

KEEPING AFLOAT

At Fifi's school every Wednesday there is an assembly which parents are invited to, and at least once a term the dashing colonel who runs the school on his own lines announces to the parents in his loud voice that no pupil has ever drowned. He also points out that no one ever saved themselves from drowning by reading a book and emphasises that it is more important for pupils to swim than to read.

Being able to swim is one way of introducing your child to a truly heavenly activity. Tiny babies can learn to swim brilliantly, toddlers regard it as a marvellous afternoon out, throwing themselves at the wave machine, sliding down water chutes, and going home completely exhausted. Older children are capable of independently swimming off and earning lots of swimming badges which you then have to sew on their trunks. Of course, I am painting a picture of watery bliss with you and your child slipping like dolphins into the deep end. The reality, I have noticed, after many hours in the water, is often shivering, slightly blue children clutching their mothers and sobbing. But if you start your child learning early enough, preferably as a baby or small toddler, and I mean small, she will not be miserable at the swimming pool.

Getting changed The first problem you will notice when you get to the pool is that most of the changing rooms are half the size of a public toilet. It is hard to get yourself, your child and the swimming bag in without your bottom hanging out of the curtain and the armbands inflated and impossible to move. (You can gradually start to decrease the amount of air in them as your child becomes more mobile in the water.) I usually use the public changing areas rather than the private ones, as there is more room, but you run the risk of a toddler passing some horribly truthful remark about your anatomy. The last time I went swimming I heard a small boy asking

his mother why another woman had red and purple stripes all over her bottom . . .

Always remember to take nappies if your child's this age. Unless it is freezing cold outside I would advocate dressing her in as few clothes as possible, because it saves time at the end when you are cold and wet. Before you go for the first time, find out what coins the lockers take and whether there are changing mats for a baby. Find out what sort of pool it is – those with a beach-style shallow end are obviously more suitable for small children.

Take it gently The first time you visit you can both loll around getting used to the water and splashing water on each other's faces. No matter what, you must remember to make your child wear armbands until she can swim really competently. It is wise to keep your early lessons in the water quite short, and make sure you're out of the water before your teeth start to chatter.

Once your child's used to the water, you can begin playing games like Chasing. 'Ring-a-ring-o'-roses' will encourage a child to put her head under water, and running in the water is a good exercise. However, warn your child never to run along the side of the pool as it can result in slipping and nasty accidents.

Afterwards When you have finished your session do not get any wild ideas about using any pool facilities. I can assure you that your own bathroom will be much more comfortable – and warmer. Do not get any ideas about luxuriating in the showers with your children. The best thing to do is to get everyone dressed and out of the changing rooms as soon as possible. Have some snacks with you so that the older ones can be kept happy while you're dressing the younger ones. If you cannot persuade your children to come out of the pool, bribery is the best strategy. Most pools have cafés, and I find that a bag of chips is the best carrot to dangle over the shallow end.

Rules of the Pool

Make sure that the pool's water temperature is at least 85° Fahrenheit (29° Centigrade).

Avoid any classes possibly originated in Siberia that involve ducking, drowning and violent dragging around of your child.

Make sure that, if you are employing a tutor, he or she is properly qualified through the Swimming Teachers' Association.

Only use armbands with two push-in air valves on each band. Avoid rubber rings, as they're not suitable for very young children.

Do not take an unwell child swimming.

Never leave a child alone by a pool.

If you're in the water helping your child to learn to swim, wear a T-shirt so that it gives her something to hold on to.

Chapter Six

Out and About

Every mother has days when she wakes up tired, and can't face the idea of taking a toddler out. What she'd really prefer is to be wrapped in lilac-scented towels and then massaged by Nubian male prostitutes rather than being poked in the groin by her buggy handle on the up-escalator in a sweaty, teeming department store. I find that it's the prospect of hauling baby, pushchair, other small children, handbag and other accoutrements around that makes me feel harassed before I've even started. There can be few things more awful than trying to hold a squirming toddler with one hand, withdrawing money for your bus fare with the other, and simultaneously attempting to fold up the pushchair and keep your tights up. This is before you've even got where you are going. Once inside a shop, a toddler will act as though she's Bill Sikes, stuffing everything she likes into her dungarees and grinning innocently at store detectives while you look for what you need and attempt to stop your child from shop-lifting entire shelves of merchandise. That said, all small children love to go out on trips, and will embrace even a short journey to the local shops with an alacrity not matched by yours! And it's essential for mothers with small children to get out and about. You're obviously going to need to shop, visit friends, maybe attend a college course, go swimming – in other words, you'll want to continue to lead an interesting existence as a parent.

The odd day in the countryside can do wonders for a city child, I suppose it's the space and air, the entirely different feeling that comes from experiencing vast areas of greenery, which just isn't the same in Battersea Park as one skips between the dog poohs. For children, a day in the country means being able to run around like mad things, shouting if they want, without bothering anyone, least of all their mother who can lie under a tree if she feels like it and not worry that they might have fallen under an articulated lorry.

Children in the country are less cheeky and less work – they are able to play outside almost all day long – a pleasure denied many town-dwellers. Children behave better because they are knackered at the end of the day, and sleep better. There are many pleasures to be had for the price of a rail ticket . . .

Having a toddler doesn't mean you can't take her abroad with you. I'm absolutely in favour of travelling with young children. I go everywhere with mine, so it's made me aware of what can go horribly wrong! However, the experience needn't be a nightmare. Because my children come everywhere with me I've had to become an efficient traveller – and I never go first class – well, not unless someone is paying for us all!

Going out with a toddler makes you realise that it's a dog's life for a child in this country. On public transport, in shops, and in cafés and restaurants, young children are expected to be silent or invisible (preferably both), and certainly not expected to be seen anywhere later than four in the afternoon. It comes as a shock to go to Italy, Spain, America or Australia, where kids are welcomed with wide-open arms. In many American restaurants, for example, high chairs are proffered along with colouring books and crayons. To be in a country where children play happily alongside their eating parents on balmy evenings is paradise. You suddenly discover that your child is a ticket to the best service, not the worst . . .

GOING OUT

Ease the burden The first thing to do is axe the pushchair if you are only dealing with one child, and purchase a sling. A hip sling is perfect for carrying a child of up to three years old, and dispenses with the problem of having to stop and look at every single solitary thing in the shop before you get to where you are going. With a sling, *you* can decide where you're going, and you can get on the bus, tube or into a taxi with ease.

I imagine you're now wondering about the hernia you'll get carrying the groceries as well. The best form of prevention seems to be a wheel-around basket, like the one your granny had.

More than two children, and you will have to succumb to a pushchair, although I've only just got one – a double one that makes me feel as though I have a litter of children rather than just three with me. With the double pushchair I have to say the ease of nipping around is slightly curtailed, mainly because I now have to Fosbury flop over the top of it to get it through the swing doors of most shops. However, I'm now convincing myself this is in fact saving me money as I only buy anything when it is truly necessary!

With a double pram and a sling, you can put the smallest baby in the sling, and all the groceries in bags on one side of the pram. But forget about getting into a London taxi for the next few years . . .

What to do if you lose each other God forbid this should happen, but it can be easy to miss a small child in a busy shop, and even a couple of minutes out of sight is enough to give any mother a seizure. It's a good idea to make sure that your child knows that she must *never* wander around and around looking for you (as she'll get more lost). Tell her to stay where she is and you'll find her; dress her in really bright clothes so she's easily spotable, and if you are very worried about her getting lost give her a whistle on a ribbon so she can contact you easily.

Braving a restaurant Eating out with under-fives can be very very trying. Behaviour that is messy but acceptable in the privacy of one's own kitchen will horrify the people at the next table and make you wonder whether they've ever seen an eighteen month old eat before. Even if your child's used to eating out with you, it's wise not to expect perfect manners. If things threaten to get completely out of hand, take your toddler outside for a few minutes to chill out and recover her temper (and give you back your equilibrium!). However, don't get brow-beaten into a migraine by hostile stares: only grumpy people expect small children to behave like paragons of virtue, and you should try to enjoy your meal with your child.

Remember to take with you a large bib; a change of T-shirt; some Wet Ones; and her favourite book or colouring book to occupy her until her food comes.

LONG JOURNEYS

Be prepared If you're going on a long journey by bus, train, or car, you need to prepare carefully. Make up lots of little bags with a snack in each. Frequent snacks help the time pass for small children, but only take food that isn't messy: fruit, sultanas, cheese, and biscuits, for example.

Take plenty of toys with you. Put each one in a paper bag, and produce a different bag every twenty minutes so as to avoid boredom.

For an older pre-schooler, a colouring book and crayons are a good idea, as are favourite song and story tapes. Nursery rhyme tapes are popular – but I'd advise you not to play them throughout the whole journey, as about an hour of these is enough to make most adults long to leap out of the moving car and escape!

Make frequent stops If you're in the car, you'll probably find that half an hour is about the limit a toddler can stand without getting bored, hungry, tired or wet, or a fascinating mixture of all four. Even a stop at a petrol station will give her a chance to get out and stretch her legs. She'll be diverted by watching you and chatting to you about it.

Play games If stuffing her face, colouring, or listening to tapes isn't enough to keep her occupied, try playing I-spy; spotting different kinds of dogs, cars, etc; singing the alphabet; or singing old hits from Broadway musicals – and then back to the biscuits for solace...

Check-list Whatever your mode of transport, don't forget your child's favourite 'comfort' toy (the one she takes to bed with her); scented plastic bags for used nappies; spare nappies; plenty of drinks in cartons; a complete change of clothing; a jumper; and a box of Wet Ones.

A word about car safety Young children are twice as likely as adults to be killed in a car accident if not fastened into a safety seat. Each year, 1,300 children are injured, and 7,000 more less seriously, while travelling by car. And yet really car safety is a simple thing – all children should be in a special child's car seat, and when they outgrow that they must have a booster seat and wear a seat belt for every trip they make, however short.

The Royal Society for the Prevention of Accidents has produced a leaflet that gives guidance on choosing the right safety harness or seat for a child. Copies are available from your local authority road safety officer, who will also be willing to give advice on car safety. Manufacturers do provide instructions for fitting seats and belts, and it is extremely important to fit the seats properly. Make sure you only buy safety equipment that has been approved to the BSI 3254 standard.

Never ever let your child get out of using her seat. An accident that just jolts adults can kill a small child.

The Royal Society for the Prevention of Accidents, Cannon Ho, Priory, Queensway, Birmingham.

How to avoid puking in the car The first thing to have in the car if your child is likely to throw up is something for her to be sick into that can then be disposed of. An ice-cream container (a big one) lined with a scented nappy sack is a perfectly good receptacle, should the worst come to the worst.

As a veteran car sickness sufferer myself, I've discovered that there are things you can do to avoid using the scented ice-cream tub! Make sure that no one mentions throwing up, or travel sickness. For some reason this seems to trigger puking in children – the mere thought that they might be ill is enough to get them going, and then it's downhill fast. Make sure that your child eats little and often, as hunger pangs definitely make anyone feeling nauseous feel worse.

Never let a child prone to car sickness read in the car, and she should also try and avoid looking down. If she drops something on the floor when she's in the car, pick it up for her. Or tie her toys to strings attached to the seats so she can retrieve them easily for herself. Finally, make sure there is fresh air in the car, and that you give your child little drinks of peppermint tea with a little honey as this can be very soothing to upset stomachs.

Flying The golden rule of air travel is don't allow your toddler to get over-tired. She is bound to be excited by the prospect of going on a plane but you should still try to persuade her to nap either in the waiting lounge or on the plane after she's eaten and had a look round. Those unused to flying tend to arrive at the airport much too early. This is *never necessary* and will only prolong the tedium for your child. No flight needs you there more than an hour before departure.

Remember to take a separate bag with the things you'll be *bound* to need for any toddler on a journey.

MAKING THE MOST OF THE PLAYGROUND

From a very early age all children adore playgrounds. They have many advantages, as long as you bear in mind some simple safety rules. Playgrounds give you and your child an excuse for a walk to and from the park; and most importantly they allow children to race around working off their excess energy and frustrations in the open air.

Playground dangers Everyone knows that most accidents occur inside the home. After the home the next culprit is roads, but what many people don't realise is that playgrounds follow roads close behind. Every year about 1,500 children under five are badly injured in their local playgrounds but these risks can be greatly reduced by parents being aware of the dangers.

The playground area should be completely screened off from any dangers such as roads or ponds, and in order to keep dogs from fouling it and creating a health hazard. Each individual play area should be clearly delineated. For example, it is extremely dangerous if the swings do not have enough room. The ground under a roundabout should be soft and the slides and climbing frames should be designed so as to avoid accidents, and the sides of the slide should be six inches high at least.

The Royal Society for the Prevention of Accidents has also devised a guide to safety in the playground called *The Play Wise Code*. You really need to keep a very close eye on a toddler in the playground because she doesn't yet know her limits, and will want to play on equipment that she's not yet ready for, giving you severe palpitations when it becomes apparent that she could fall through all the gaps in the rope ladder and that she's getting rigor mortis at the top of the slide while a seething pile of eight year olds mounts the stairs at the back.

Start a playground playgroup If you have several friends with small children, why not get together. Apart from using the usual playground equipment you could organise some games outside the playground. The children could also share a snack and a story in the park, which would prolong the valuable time spent out of doors. The Pre-School Playgroups Association gives advice on how to set up your own playgroup.

Bring along some lining paper so that everyone can draw a self-portrait. Take the opportunity to observe a bit of nature together – even if it's only an overweight duck!

The Pre-School Playgroups Association, 314 Vauxhall Bridge Road, London SW1V 1AA.

PICNICS

For a parent feeling claustrophobic at home, the picnic is the world's finest invention! It's also perfect if you just want to while away an afternoon gazing at big white clouds scudding across the blue skies as your child, or children, run riot near by. In the summer I pack a picnic lunch for Fifi and her gang almost every day and send them off into the further reaches of the garden to eat it. In fact, it's probably one of the things that Fifi will hold against me later in life when she becomes a dungaree-wearing militant feminist. She'll remind me that in the summer I wouldn't allow any of the children back into the house until five o'clock, which meant they had to entertain themselves outdoors all afternoon, regardless of the vagaries of the English weather. She'll look back with derision at my belief that children should get plenty of air on their bodies instead of spending the entire time shrouded in semi-darkness watching cartoons on TV...

Food for picnics Usually you can count on having to walk a certain distance as you search for the perfect spot, so it's a good idea not to take mountains of luggage requiring the services of Sherpa Tenzing just to get you up a small hillock. Take food that you know your child is going to enjoy, instead of mounds of food that she ends up not eating. If there *is* anything left over, feed it to the birds, but remember never to leave rubbish in the countryside. Cold sausages; cucumber sticks; crisps; fruit; raw carrots; biscuits; cakes and small sandwiches are all a success, I've found, and mean that you don't have to fiddle around with plates or cutlery.

Drinks I'd take little cartons of juice as they are easiest to carry – and for younger ones a big bottle of watered-down juice so that you can keep bottles and beakers topped up all day – there's nothing worse than gasping for a drink after furiously running about and discovering that there's nothing left to swill. Freeze the bottle of juice before you go, and put it in with the food to keep the food cool.

Picnic equipment Always take a big rug to lie on and an old tablecloth for the food – one that you don't mind wrecking with grass stains. You could even use an old towel so that the children can wipe their hands on it as well as sit on it! Try and avoid traditional hampers as they bump into your legs when you carry them and half-cripple you, and anyway weigh a ton. In your plastic bag take Wet Ones, a knife, and a rubbish bag for the return journey – but lightness is the name of the game. Try not to leave anything behind!

Outdoor games and activities One of the things you can do while you are out is collect pretty leaves to press when you get back home. If you take some paper and fat crayons with you, the children can do bark rubbings on the trees you pass. Simply put the paper on the tree and crayon over it until the pattern comes through. A word of warning! When your child is collecting natural treasures, *make extremely sure* that nothing poisonous gets stuffed into her mouth.

For little children outdoor games need to be non-competitive and fairly short. Singing and dancing games like 'Here We Go Round the Mulberry Bush' will go down well at your picnic.

Or all sit together in a circle and sing nursery rhymes, have stories, or play hand-games like Incy wincy spider climbed up the spout, This little piggy and Pat-a-cake.

A picnic on the tube Feeling isolated, longing for a chat, wanting to go to a museum or see an exhibition and dreading the journey? Have you ever contemplated having a picnic on the tube? No one's pretending a tube journey is fun with small children, but you can make it more entertaining. Take your feast with you and eat it on the tube and the journey will pass in no time.

A seaside picnic The seaside is a dream place for a picnic. Sadly, many British beaches are polluted, so it's wise to check first before you allow your toddler near the water. Once you've found a good beach, the two of you can play ball, try your hand at Frisbee and bury each other in the sand. You'll go home loaded with feathers, little pieces of driftwood, mussel shells and dead crabs, if the two of you have been observant. Don't forget to take sunhats and sunscreen lotion if it's a hot day.

Last summer we had lots of days by the sea. A gang of children would descend on our house and we'd set off for the beach. First, the children would paddle and inspect the rock pools, finding crabs both dead and alive. One time, I bought a whole crab from a seashore shanty and we ate it on the pebbles. I have to admit I succumbed to a trampolining session after that (mainly because I thought it would knacker everyone before bedtime). When we got home we made a vast undersea collage, painted pebbles, and tried to get rid of the sand that had got into our every orifice.

A teddy bear's picnic Share this with other mothers and children, as it's more fun to be in a group. Ask all the children to bring their favourite bear, and get their mums to tie a label round its neck with their phone number on it, in case of disaster whereby *numero uno* teddy gets lost in a ditch.

Take along food on the teddy bear theme: make teddy bear-shaped sandwiches with a biscuit cutter – peanut butter and banana are our favourites. Before you go, help your child to make the Cheesy Bread Bears and the Teddy Bear Biscuits (see Chapter Three) to take with you.

Once the picnic is underway you can play Hunt the teddy, and sing 'The Teddy Bear's Picnic'.

If you find that the weather's wet on the day that you planned to have your big adventure, hold the teddy bear's picnic under the kitchen table instead. Organise teddy colouring and drawing contests, with sweets as prizes for everyone.

HOLIDAYS

Taking a holiday with a pre-schooler means that you'll probably have to re-think your concept of what a holiday is! The under-five brigade have little interest in sunbathing, no interest in sightseeing, and a huge capacity for boredom.

Share a holiday Toddlers adore playing on the beach, swimming and paddling, so if you don't fancy an entire holiday with a bucket and spade by your side you might contemplate taking a well-loved auntie or friend along. Or you could consider taking a holiday with another couple with children which is another way of lessening the burden of incessant playing and entertaining. If you are sharing accommodation, it's not wise to share a car, as this would mean everyone being squashed in together and you wouldn't be able to zip off somewhere separately if you got the urge.

A self-catering holiday This is popular among families with little children, but I always think that's a bit of a swizz for mothers because they still have to cook and wash up just like they do at home.

A holiday in Britain Now that global warming is turning most of Britain into a tropical paradise (by the turn of the century any mum going to Gerrards Cross will be dressed like Dorothy Lamour) many families are opting for holidays in this country, which are cheaper and less hassle from a travelling point of view.

Lots of farms as well as hotels cater for families with young children; a house-swap is another possibility.

PICKING YOUR OWN FRUIT

A blissful pursuit Anyone who has read the Larkin books by H. E. Bates will have spent wistful moments visualising the idyllic English activity that is more commonly known as picking your own. There is nothing quite like a hot day spent in the open, picking delicious strawberries with the scent of haystacks and honeysuckle in your nostrils, and the atmosphere so quiet that all you can hear is the sound of the birds. Not that you have to be a Larkin to enjoy this characteristically British summer activity. One of the favourite pursuits of Fifi, Peaches and Pixie is to pick fruit at a farm near where we live in Kent, although they seem to eat more raspberries and strawberries than they put in the punnet! The farm has recently acquired a huge, charmingly rustic adventure playground. Another large area is entirely devoted to young animals: calves, ponies, rabbits and pigs, all of which the children are allowed to feed with special bags of food that cost 50p each from the shop. The shop also sells Devil's Cottage Cream and useful aids to country living like feather dusters and fly papers.

Where You can pick your own fruit at farms all over the country. A visit to such a farm makes the perfect day out for town-dwellers, who may otherwise never see a raspberry except in a freezer cabinet. The Farm Shop and Pick Your Own Association publishes a free guide to pick-your-own facilities throughout Britain. The guide details which fruit (and vegetables) are available and where, as well as listing other amenities and entertainments like picnic and refreshment areas, playgrounds, farmyard animals and nature rambles.

The Farm Shop and Pick Your Own Association, Agriculture House, Knightsbridge, London SW1X 7NJ.

Chapter Seven

Throwing a Bash

I loathe most adult parties. I'm invariably the one who's over-dressed, and ends up sitting on the stairs outside the only loo at the party with my best friend, moaning about how no men find me attractive now I've got fifteen children, and being continually stepped over, in their haste to do something about their bursting bladders, by far too pretty girls in black Lycra dresses.

But I adore all children's parties, especially ours! Children's parties can celebrate anything from a birthday to a special date on the calendar like Hallowe'en or Bonfire Night. Alternatively, you could throw a theme party: we had one where everyone came dressed as a bee, but you could be even more imaginative if you have the inclination to do an extra bit of preparation. We're thinking of having a Kylie Minogue party next.

Why should you bother with theme parties? Because they are such fun for so little effort, and your children will be thrilled, and probably never forget them. Personally, I think a party should be conjured up every six weeks – which is perfectly possible if you think hard enough!

There are many books available detailing the process of arrang-ing and executing the successful party, but what I'm going to pass on here are a few tips I've gleaned from personal experience, in fact, eight years of party-throwing for the under-three-foot set ...

START BY AVOIDING THE PARTY BLUES

The bad news about parties for youngsters is that if things go wrong children are not reticent about making their feelings felt (unlike adults who end up quietly blubbing in a corner with mascara running and boob tube at half mast). You may find that the combination of disappointment and over-excitement, or excess sugar and getting over-heated – or all four – leaves the apple of your eye bawling her eyes out and you feeling cross because you've done all this preparation just for her, and she seems to be hating every minute of it.

Prevent breakages and squabbles Hide precious breakable objects, and put away any special toys that your child would be unwilling to share with a marauding herd of toddler friends.

Keep the numbers down Don't be tempted to have too many guests, especially if your space is limited. Too many children leads to chaos, and near-tropical heat in the kitchen. Your small-fry will begin to think that they're inhabiting a madhouse. One solution is to hold the party in a local park. Whatever the number of guests, try and enlist some adult friends to help.

Don't have too much rich food Eat first, and remember that, although most parties are a great excuse for children to stuff themselves with every additive ever invented with a lot of sugar on the top, party food doesn't have to be unhealthy. Try and prepare a table that has savouries like sausages on sticks and fish fingers. It may not seem very festive, but at least it provides an alternative to 'bad' foods. Another thing to bear in mind is that, apart from the cake, you may be able to get away with having no other sugary food. Health food shops stock all manner of natural carob sweets, fruit rolls and various other delicious things that will not send your children bouncing off the walls within twenty minutes of eating them.

Keep it calm Try not to let your child become over-excited before the event. A modicum of excitement is inevitable but don't let the preparations go *on and on* until you all end up feeling as though you're launching another space shuttle, not having a simple bash. Persuade someone to read a story to the guests during tea, as this soothes everyone before the games start.

Keep it simple Try not to expect too much of your party – some good games, plenty of giggling, a few gifts and enough food is all that is necessary for under-fives. You don't have to kill yourself in the process.

Presents If it's a birthday party, I think it's best to set aside a place where everyone leaves their presents. That way, the birthday girl can open them quietly when everything is over, instead of in a frenzy of paper-ripping, with a glazed look on her face, resolutely forgetting to say thank you once, and turning into someone you hope never to meet again. Make sure you write a list of who gave what, ready for thank-you letter time.

Wind down afterwards It's important that after the party you have a good long time being quiet together – looking at the presents, or just discussing the events of the afternoon.

Keep it short Did I say afternoon? One of the secrets of a good party is knowing when to call a halt to it. When you send out the invitations, make it *clear* when you expect parents to pick children up so that the party doesn't become a marathon. I've found that for the under-five set two hours of near-frenzy is *ample*. Keep all the guests' phone numbers at hand, should a parent be late in picking up a child, or in the event of a child being taken ill or becoming very upset.

GOOD PREPARATION

Invitations Decide who to invite, remembering to curb your child's natural desire to invite everyone, including the midwife who delivered her. Send out invitations in good time; your child could illustrate these – it's more fun, and cheaper! Alternatively, phone the children's parents to speed things up, if your party is an impromptu affair. Tie balloons to your front door on D-Day so guests can find you!

Food Make up your mind well in advance what food you're going to serve – you can have a thrilling party with just crisps, cake and jelly, if you want to keep costs down. Or you might want something on a theme like a pumpkin-shaped cake for Hallowe'en, or perhaps pizzas in their boxes (which saves having to clear up, if that's what you're dreading!). Whatever food you decide upon, make sure it doesn't require a lot of elaborate cooking, and serve it where it won't matter if it gets spilt.

Remember that your helpers will stuff themselves as well as helping, so you'll need more food for them. Marmite, mashed banana and honey are popular with adults and children alike. At one of our parties, all the children tucked into blue cheese and the adults ate the banana sandwiches, becoming misty-eyed with nostalgia for their childhood parties as the toddlers breathed totally noxious fumes over each other during Pass the parcel. If your child is under three, then her friends' parents will probably want to stay around at the party, tucking into your jellies with a vengeance. If the party's for an older child, then parents will leave their children with you. While a load of four year olds descending on you for the afternoon may seem a thoroughly offputting idea, it could pay dividends. Once parents have seen the thrilling fun to be had at your place, they'll follow suit and you'll have a free afternoon to have your legs waxed, or mowed, as the case may be after several years with an under-five.

Entertainers If you'd like to hire a magician or a clown for the party, be clear about how long you want them to perform for so that they don't take over completely.

Games Stick to non-competitive games and have gold stars to stick on to everyone. Don't feel you have to give out elaborate prizes: bags of sweets or home-made biscuits will go down just as well as a full-scale Barbie swimming pool. Make sure that the party girl wins a game (alongside everyone else!) and doesn't end up feeling left out of her own party as a result of your efforts to be the hostess with the mostest.

Bear in mind, when planning the number of games, that little children wee all the time. Regular trips to the toilet by the guests will interrupt the proceedings!

Games are an important part of an under-fives' party, so you need to plan them beforehand. They mustn't be complicated or the children will simply get bored and fractious, and you will get a pain in the groin from trying to gee everyone up after the dismal failure of your under-threes' chess tournament. Here are some suggestions: Simon says; Hunt the thimble (or sweets); Pass the parcel (when we played this at Fifi's last party, each layer of paper had a present in it, and when the music stopped each child got the chance to unwrap the parcel and find a gift); Musical statues; Musical balloons (put one balloon per child in a pile in the middle of the room and remove one balloon each time the music stops. The winner is the last one left holding a balloon); Blindfolded tasting (put peanut butter, orange segments etc on to small saucers, blindfold the children, and get them to take turns at identifying the food by tasting it); Throwing a beanbag (accurately!) into a basket; Musical chairs. Very small children will want to play their favourite singing games at the party, like 'Oranges and Lemons' and 'The Farmer's in His Den'.

Going home time If you want to give out party bags at the end, you could make this into a treasure hunt, only don't make finding them too difficult or the children will be there all night ... Then it's coats on, and home for all the exhausted, exhilarated little guests, puce in the face and with hair covered in jelly . . .

Photographs Don't forget to get plenty of film for your camera, because you'll want to record the happy event.

A CHRISTMAS PARTY

Make the most of the season Christmas parties should be held at least a couple of weeks before Christmas to allow parents a chance to do some Christmas shopping! Apart from this noble reason, the other one is that you don't want your child to become Christmassed out with too much happening at once.

Christmas parties are the easiest ones of all to arrange – the tree will already be there (in our house we have to restrain ourselves from putting the tree up in September). The decorations will be up, and if they aren't you can get all the children to make them, in between playing games. Because there is so much you can do around the theme of Christmas, a party at this time of the year can last longer than usual without anyone getting cheesed off or fractious.

Food Try to keep it simple because if you're planning to help guests make Christmassy things that will be quite enough to contend with! A big Christmas cake with the usual model snowmen, trees, children in sleighs and Santas on top, large glasses of milk, and maybe a cheese and tomato pizza will suffice, you'll find, and won't be too much trouble to prepare. Another suggestion is a big batch of Christmas tree-shaped biscuits – one for each guest with her name piped on it with icing.

Party bags and prizes Don't forget the golden rule of little kids' parties: *everyone* has to win something! Give additional Christmas tree biscuits; or gingerbread men and women or stockings with the children's names stuck on with glitter; or simply give sweets.

Santa Claus Once the children have played the usual games and sung endless rounds of Christmas carols and songs, you could arrange for Dad to arrive dressed as Santa Claus. You'll certainly need film in your camera for this because everyone's mum and dad will want a picture of their angel discussing with Santa the likelihood of getting a bazooka for Christmas.

Simple festive handicrafts Very young children could manage paper chains, or they could draw and paint their own Christmas cards to take home. If you're going to make these, have plenty of children's glue at hand so that each child can liberally apply cotton-wool snow and glitter to their finished pictures.

Or try Christmas tree decorations ... The simplest ones can be made from cutting star or tree shapes out of cardboard, and making a small hole at the top to thread the string through to hang them up by. The decorations can then be painted, or covered with hundreds and thousands, glitter, cotton wool or confetti. Alternatively, you could cut up old Christmas cards and decorate the existing pictures. Or the children could make gingerbread decorations. Give each child a ball of raw gingerbread dough for her to shape. Bake the shapes while everyone plays more games, or makes something else.

Egg cup bells are easy to make and look pretty on the Christmas tree. Cut up an egg carton so that all the egg-containers are separate. Cover them with kitchen foil, and pierce a hole in the bottom for the thread.

Something more ambitious Older pre-schoolers could try making a Christmas wreath for the door. Each child will need a large cardboard circle (do this before the party begins or you'll find yourself spending the entire party chopping at lumps of card). The card must be thick and strong. Once each child is armed with glue and a hole has been made at the top ready for a red ribbon, she's ready to stick on pine cones, nuts, and anything else you've managed to find in the garden that looks festive. Wreaths should be allowed to dry out overnight before enthusiastic parents hang them up, otherwise your nuts will drop off...

More artistry To make stained glass windows you need thick black paper for the window frame and some transparent paper (cellophane or coloured tracing paper) for the stained glass. First, stick

see-through sweet wrappers and coloured tissue paper on to the cellophane sheets. Then glue the frame on to the cellophane square. The children could hang the frames up in their bedroom windows.

A cautionary tale Last Christmas I set to work with Fifi and several of her friends (they were seven at the time) making Yule logs, with real logs which the children sprayed with silver glitter, covered in cotton wool, and stuck model robins from the local newsagent on to. At one end was a red satin ribbon, at the other, a fat red candle – the finished logs intended to be a glorious centrepiece for the family Christmas dinner table. Sadly, things went awry and my usual alertness to all possible safety hazards failed. Simon, aged nine, who lives next door, lit his candle and the cotton wool was set on fire, rapidly spreading to the entire log. Simon's log was flung into the sink and we had to start again, *minus the red candles* . . .

An Advent box hanging Again, this is something for older children to make, but it's fun for everyone in the family when it's finished. Collect small cereal cartons, matchboxes etc – quite a lot, so that there are enough to go round. Cover a coat-hanger with ribbon or wrapping paper, and tie a big satin bow at the top. Fill each box with a tiny toy or trinket, a sweet, or a chocolate bar, and wrap each little present up. Tie a long length of ribbon round each little box and tie the boxes to the coat-hanger. Label each box with a number – from 1 to 24. The children can count the days leading up to Christmas by opening a little box each day. It's a nice alternative to the Advent calendar, and children love the element of surprise as they open their little boxes. The hanging looks wonderfully festive, too – a mass of ribbons, bows, presents, and curly bits . . .

AN EASTER PARTY

Food The main thing that stands out in my mind about Easter parties is the opportunity they give you to persuade children to eat lettuce in large amounts under the guise of rabbit salad. It's fun to expand on the rabbit theme – try making a rabbit-shaped jelly on a bed of green-jelly grass, or a rabbit-shaped cake covered with desiccated coconut fur.

Decorations These are easy: rabbits (!) in any shape or form, Easter chicks, rabbit ears for the guests, egg-shaped hangings here and there and bunches of daffodils all over the place to give that spring-like air.

The Egg hunt This should be the main party game, and needs to be set up in advance, although once I completely forgot to hide the eggs and had to shut two bewildered guests into the spare bedroom while I furtively ran round stuffing little eggs into every corner of the house and garden. Remember not to make the hiding places too difficult or the children will be looking for the next year.

Decorate eggs If you want to have activities as well as games and the hunt, decorating eggs is a good one that can go on for some time. You'll need to keep your table well covered with both a large towel and some newspapers. Provide the guests with plenty of hardboiled eggs, and some food colouring. Either use the manufactured food colouring or use beetroot juice (red), soaked red-cabbage leaves (blue), and cold coffee (brown). Once the children have drawn a design or scribbly pattern in crayon on to their hardboiled egg, they are ready to dip the egg into a cool solution of food colouring. They'll have to do the dunking with a spoon unless you want them to have permanently lime-green and magenta hands. Once the egg is a strong enough colour, it is ready to be left to dry on a wrinkly bit of tin foil. Encourage guests to take their decorated eggs home with them to eat.

The children might like to make little baskets filled with chopped-up tissue-paper grass to put the eggs into. Any small container will do. Cover it with slightly crinkled-up tin foil, and then decorate the baskets with powder paint that has a little washing-up liquid added to it so that the paint sticks to the foil. Make the basket handles out of crêpe paper or thick wool.

Easter bonnets If all this egg activity seems a bit messy perhaps you'd feel more inclined to try these. A hat can either be made out of the simple cardboard cone or by adding ribbons to a large paper plate (see Chapter One). The children can then paint the hats, stick on Easter chicks and paper flowers, and have a parade around the garden!

Easter games You could try Pass the Easter chick instead of the parcel. If you've got a garden, an egg and spoon race allows for some running up and down and letting off of steam!

A HALLOWE'EN PARTY

Ghoulish decorations There's a lot of scope here! Create a ghost for the corner of the room by draping a sheet over the kitchen brush and gluing in two eyes. Swing plastic bats from the ceiling lamps, and spray cobwebs all over the place, all of which will create a splendidly spookiferous atmosphere!

Games and activities You don't have to go trick or treating (in London this seems to be fairly common but in deepest Norwich, for example, I can't imagine that the streets are alive with trick or treaters). You may feel that you and your merry band of small children are better off playing Pin the hat on the witch, and Feel the witch's brew (a bowl filled with pumpkin seeds). Even if you are not going out, though, it's a party that calls for costumes – cats, ghosts and witches are all the obvious order of the day.

Instead of carving your pumpkin into a night light before the party, you could do the carving just before you serve the food, so that the candle can be lit and the pumpkin placed in the centre of the table while the children watch.

The children could draw Hallowe'en pictures, or make Hallowe'en faces out of an orange cup cake and lots of sultanas. Bob the apple is wildly popular, or try a Hallowe'en scavenger hunt – Hunt the bat, or the witch's hat, or just a bar of chocolate. Give *everyone* a toffee apple prize for effort . . .

Paula Yates
The Fun Starts Here £5.99

After her first baby was born, the most frequent question Paula Yates was asked was simply: How can you *survive* motherhood, let alone *enjoy* it?

The Fun Starts Here is her ecstatic, encouraging and eminently practical response – a personal guide to every joy a baby can bring.

'Paula is the real thing. Truly a mother who knows about the "amazing technicolour world of babies' nappies" and of the great joy of gently nibbling on a baby's bottom.' POLLY SAMSON, SUNDAY TIMES

'She has merely pointed out that there is an alternative for working mothers . . . we should be grateful to Miss Yates.'
EMMA SOAMES, EVENING STANDARD

'Very funny . . . very useful . . . a great present for a pregnant friend.'
OXFORD MAIL

'Personal and positive . . . a passionate hymn to life in the home.'
VICTORIA WHITE, IRISH TIMES

'A positive celebration as well as a practical guide to pregnancy, birth and baby-care.' SUZANNE MOORE, CITY LIMITS

Gordon Bourne, FRCS, FRCOG
Pregnancy £7.99

Having a child can be one of the most exciting and fulfilling experiences in a woman's life, provided she and her partner have the confidence that comes from knowing exactly what pregnancy involves.

Pregnancy is *the* complete and comprehensive guide. Written by Gordon Bourne, a leading consultant obstetrician and gynaecologist, it provides essential information, guidance and reassurance on all aspects of pregnancy and childbirth.

'The most authoritative and comprehensive guide to pregnancy, labour and motherhood.' VOGUE

'Few baby books will tell a quarter of the mysteries the good but authoritarian Gordon Bourne unfolds here.' THE GUARDIAN

'Comprehensive and authoritative.' WOMEN'S WEEKLY

'Sets out in a clear, factual and reassuring way every possible aspect of pregnancy . . . I would recommend this book to anyone who can buy or borrow a copy.' MARRIAGE GUIDANCE

'Very useful . . . expectant fathers would do well to read this one too.' WOMAN'S OWN

D. C. Jarvis M.D.
Folk Medicine £3.99

Health Secrets which can prolong life and give vigour to young and old . . .

The late Dr Jarvis lived and practised among the tough mountain folk of Vermont for over fifty years. This unique and remarkable book – which has sold over 500,000 copies in the Pan edition alone – is the result of his deep study of their way of life, and in particular of their concept of diet and time-honoured folk medicine.

It offers a novel theory on the treatment and prevention of a wide range of diseases and nagging complaints:

THE COMMON COLD
HAY FEVER
ARTHRITIS
KIDNEY TROUBLE
DIGESTIVE DISORDERS
OVERWEIGHT
HIGH BLOOD PRESSURE
CHRONIC FATIGUE

and many others which often defy conventional diagnosis and treatment.

'There is not a family in the land who won't find its theories – and propositions – fascinating.' DAILY EXPRESS

Dr Peter Hanson
The Joy of Stress £5.99

How to make pressure work for you

Stess can be positive – when you know how to handle it!

Dr Peter Hanson has developed a unique method of making the most of
the stresses in our lives: when to challenge them, when to control them
and when to ignore them. Simple and fun to use, it shows how you can
survive and thrive on stress – by making it work for you.

The Hanson Method is a rewarding and exciting route to better health and
personal success. It is a ready-to-use plan which will work immediately and
last a lifetime. Illustrated with diagrams and cartoons, Dr Hanson gives his
practical advice with a rare combination of genuine medical insight and
humour.

The Joy of Stress shows how to enjoy the thrills of stress – by leaving the
threat behind.

Coach Jim Everroad
How to Flatten Your Stomach £1.99

It's quick, it's smple . . . and it can work for you!

An effective figure and fitness programme, devised by an expert with over 20 different exercises clearly illustrated and explained. Only a few minutes a day will rapidly flatten your stomach, making you feel and look good!

It's so easy that anyone can do it!

All Pan books are available at your local bookshop or newsagent, or can be ordered direct from the publisher. Indicate the number of copies required and fill in the form below.

Send to: Pan C. S. Dept
            Macmillan Distribution Ltd
            Houndmills Basingstoke RG21 2XS
or phone: 0256 29242, quoting title, author and Credit Card number.

Please enclose a remittance* to the value of the cover price plus: £1.00 for the first book plus 50p per copy for each additional book ordered.

*Payment may be made in sterling by UK personal cheque, postal order, sterling draft or international money order, made payable to Pan Books Ltd.

Alternatively by Barclaycard/Access/Amex/Diners

Card No. ☐☐☐☐☐☐☐☐☐☐☐☐☐☐☐☐☐☐

Expiry Date ☐☐☐☐☐☐

Signature:

Applicable only in the UK and BFPO addresses

While every effort is made to keep prices low, it is sometimes necessary to increase prices at short notice. Pan Books reserve the right to show on covers and charge new retail prices which may differ from those advertised in the text or elsewhere.

NAME AND ADDRESS IN BLOCK LETTERS PLEASE:

....

Name _____

Address _____

_____

_____

_____

6/92